# OUTLINES OF CHURCH HISTORY

Rudolf Sohm (1841-1917) was Professor of Law at Gottingen, Freiberg, Strasbourg and Leipzig Universities in the period from 1870 to 1900. He was the author of several books on church and legal history. English translations of his works include *The Institutes of Roman Law, A History of Christianity,* and the present volume.

# OUTLINES
# OF CHURCH HISTORY

*By* RUDOLF SOHM

*Translated by* MAY SINCLAIR

*With a Preface by* H. M. GWATKIN

*Introduction by* JAMES LUTHER ADAMS

BEACON PRESS     BEACON HILL     BOSTON

# EDITOR'S PREFACE

THE present work is intended to supply a want which most historical teachers must have felt—that of a clear and suggestive outline of general Church History for intelligent readers.   Such a manual is Professor Rudolf Sohm's *Kirchengeschichte im Grundriss*.   Short as it is, it is neither a meagre sketch nor a confused mass of facts, but a masterly outline of Church History from the first ages to our own times, combining a lawyer's precision and a historian's insight into the meaning of events with a philosopher's sense of the unity of history and a Christian's conviction that the Kingdom of God is spiritual.

The translation is made from the eighth German edition, which the author has brought well up to date. His vigorous and often epigrammatic sentences are far from easy to render into flowing English, and the work has cost the accomplished translator no little time and care.

We are becoming used to the transformation of Christian thought by the advance of science during the last two hundred years.   It has been 'a revelation come up from the earth to meet the revelation which had come down from heaven' (Hort). It may be that another revelation is coming back from the past which will work another and as great a transformation in the next two hundred years. The critical study of history has already done much to loosen our Pharisaic ideas of the Gospel, and to show that it is far more spiritual than Catholic or Calvinist imagined. It has revealed a new world, which is yet an old one, of Christian thought beyond and above the narrow Western sectarianism which bounded the horizon of Catholics, and even of Protestants also. Not by unreasoning worship of the past, nor by ignorant contempt of it, nor yet by partisan distortion of it, but by critical and sympathetic study of it, we shall learn something of the grandeur of our own time, and of the meaning of the mighty questions which lie before our children.

H. M. GWATKIN.

# AUTHOR'S PREFACE

THE following pages contain a collection of essays which I published some little time ago in the *Allgemeine Conservative Monatsschrift*. It is not without some misgiving that I now bring these essays out as a whole. Yet I dare to hope that this method of exposition, by which I attempt to present the history of the Church as a part of universal history, will perhaps make it easier for the casual reader to obtain a survey of the whole course of historical development, and an insight into those spiritual forces which through Christianity have flowed out into the world.

LEIPZIG, *November 12th*, 1887.

The Second Edition differs from the first only in a few alterations.

LEIPZIG, *February 14th*, 1888.

A few additions have been made to the Third Edition; as in § 10, Montanism; § 15, Rise of Monasticism—Augustine. But the work as a whole has remained unchanged.

LEIPZIG, *November 8th*, 1888.

The Fourth Edition was unchanged from the third. The opportunity offered by a Fifth Edition is taken to revise the whole carefully once more, and to enlarge it by some additions which seemed necessary in order to present the whole picture in a clearer light. With this view sections 6, 7, 16, 20, 26, 32, and 51 have undergone fresh treatment with reference to the 'Proceedings against the Christians,' Iconoclasm, the *Libri Carolini*, Pope Nicolas I., Bernard of Clairvaux, 'Reforming Forces,' and Alphonso of Liguori.

LEIPZIG, *January* 19*th*, 1890.

In the Eighth Edition some sections, namely §§ 10-38, have been further elaborated with special reference to the results set forth in my *Ecclesiastical Law*, vol. i. (1892).

LEIPZIG, *February* 22*nd*, 1893.

RUDOLF SOHM

# INTRODUCTION

The first edition of *Outlines of Church History* was published over seventy years ago. Apart from Adolf Harnack's *History of Dogma,* no history of Christianity written in that period is today so widely read as Sohm's. Why is this so?

In answering this question one should not ignore the imaginative power and epigram of Sohm's style of writing. His language is in familiar vernacular; it is not technical. More than that, it achieves an eloquent flow that submerges complex detail in favor of the general idea and that epitomizes that significant tendency in symbolic incident or in Dantean simile.

Sohm's style, however, is more than a matter of lucid diction and forceful eloquence. It is informed by an interpretation of the history of Christianity which gives it the quality and stature of epic. Sohm presents the history of the church as a part of general history. For this task he was uniquely equipped. He was a jurist as well as a church historian, a historian of Roman and Frankish law as well as of Canon Law. At the same time he was a man of vigorous piety. Possessing a wide range of learning and aware of the complexity of religion in history, he sought to grasp the interrelations between idea, personality, class, and institution. Moreover, he viewed Christian faith as the lodestar of the spiritual pilgrimage of the West. "No other religion," he affirms, "has had power to guide the progress of our culture save Christianity alone. Therefore it has conquered. On its side were neither Roman legions nor ancient learning, but the power of divine truth which is mightier than all the powers of earthly life. By virtue of the spirit which is alive within her, the Christian Church in its slow upward growth had power to outlast the great Roman Empire, to join the ancient to the modern world, and to be the educator of the race of men that was to come." Of the working of this spirit through and against earthly powers Sohm makes an epic.

This epic is of a struggle that was not made without dust and heat. It is not a simple success story, for the struggle was against principalities and powers. Much of Sohm's narrative deals with apostasy and perversion and the struggle against them. The spirit alive in the churches, he says, has won its victories in spite of the fact that it has been "so miserably represented" by the adherents of Christianity. The perversions and enemies of Christian faith appear and reappear with devilish relentlessness. In kind they are small in number. They are, in the main, coercion from within and without the churches, ecclesiasticism, dogmatism, scholastic speculation about divine things, and legalism. These perversions and enemies appear in both Catholic and Protestant forms of "piety."

In face of these perversions Sohm insists that every man must do his own believing; the object of faith is not a visible church or a fixated doctrine; this object also is not amenable to rational penetration; and law in the church, when made constitutive, issues in a deception that offers man self-manufactured salvation and in a resistance to the mysterious working of the divine. Sohm points to the antidote for these perversions when he says, "It is not our culture that will save us, but the Gospel alone." All of these earthly powers can blind men to the justification that comes through faith alone. So speaks Sohm with Luther. "Life and blessedness come not by the knowledge of the world,

but by the forgiveness of sins." In short, Sohm's epic is a
Lutheran epic.

Of the earthly powers that invade the church, the most
seductive, according to Sohm, is law. It may be a law
with respect to organization or with respect to doctrine,
and it may be Catholic or Protestant. But faith in Jesus
Christ gives "deliverance from slavish service of the law,"
from coercion, from *bondage* to the past, from ultimate
reliance on human contrivance. The Christian churches
are in constant danger of "falling" away from the Gospel
into law, from life into death.

The initial "fall" of the church was the "fall" into a
legal organization, into a monarchical bureaucratic machinery providing legal tenure of office, and issuing finally in
papal infallibility. This "fall" was occasioned by the problems attendant upon the administration of the sacraments.
Sohm's account of this process is set forth at length in his
work, *Kirchenrecht* (Canon Law). At the outset the Christian churches were under the leadership of *persons* imbued
with the Holy Spirit, then these persons were subsumed
under *offices,* and the offices in turn were assigned control
of the sacraments (*or things*). This process of decline from
the leadership of Spirit to the objective bureaucratic control of things found its concomitant and sanction in the
legalization of Christianity. Precisely this process of
materialization and routinization shows that "ecclesiastical
law contradicts the nature of the church."

This conception of the "fall" of the church as its
legalization, coming as it does from Sohm the jurist, presents us with a striking paradox. As a jurist Sohm viewed
the law and legal institutions as the principal beneficent
means of secular social control. But when he turned to the
study of primitive Christianity he found in it a power and
authority that could in no way be viewed as legal. Sohm

the jurist, with his Lutheran dualism between Gospel and
law, felt that the decisively non-juridical essence in Christianity must be safeguarded against the intrusion of law.
We need not here enter into the detail of Sohm's writings
which deal with the organization of early Christianity
and with the subsequent changes. But we should give some
further indication of the Lutheran thrust of his interpretation.

The early Christians having been delivered from the
law through faith in Christ, their church had no legal
constitution. The *Ecclesia* of the first century was under
the authority of gifts of grace (*charismata*). This authority
expressed itself spontaneously in the response to the Holy
Spirit, both in the interpretation of the Word and in the
celebration of the sacraments. Thus the authority was
charismatic and not legal. The leaders had no legal right
of tenure; they were expected by the congregation to
possess charismatic gifts. Accordingly, the government
of the church was not a democracy, rule by the people; it
was a pneumatocracy, response to Spirit. The fall away
from the rule of Spirit was a sign of "small faith," of
reliance upon the false security of human devices and
upon the outward pomp and ceremony of a legally constituted and bureaucratized church. This "small faith" opened
the way for the development of Canon Law. The reliance
upon false security and upon the "power" of outward
show was an expression of man's rebellion from God; in
short, an expression of original sin. "The natural man is a
born Catholic." The resort to law, in Sohm's view, constituted the secularization of Christianity. It remained for
Luther to restore the church to reliance upon grace and
upon justification by faith, rather than upon law. Accordingly, he burned the Canon Law. But this Reformation was
not destined to remain intact. The "natural-born Catholic"

in men led the Lutheran churches again to "fall" into law.
And so the struggle continues against "small faith."

Many Lutheran scholars, like Karl Holl and Hans von
Campenhausen, will not accept Sohm's account of primitive Christianity nor his heavy emphasis on charismatic
authority. Indeed, numerous scholars have disputed his
characterization of authority in the primitive church. This
characterization, it is pointed out, ignores the dynastic
authority in the church at Jerusalem; it also overlooks the
role of tradition which may have been established initially
by charismatic authority. Adolf Harnack, holding that
constitutional regulation appeared in the church from the
beginning, long ago entered into controversy with Sohm,
though he conceded the persuasiveness of Sohm's account.
More recently Rudolf Bultmann and Emil Brunner, in
differing and limited ways, have given support to Sohm's
emphasis on charismatic authority. But Karl Barth has
now entered the lists against Brunner (whom he calls
a disciple of Sohm), insisting as a Calvinist that in the
church there must be law — "living law." Sohm himself,
it should be noted, is scarcely consistent in this matter.
In the later chapters of the *Outlines* he extols confessional-
ism and the strong organziation of an established church,
though of course he wishes to make room in the church for
charismatic authority.

As touching the whole discussion of charisma and law,
we should observe here that Max Weber the sociologist
has appropriated and expanded Sohm's conception of the
types of authority. Max Weber's typology of authority —
traditional, legal, and charismatic — presupposes Sohm's
characterization of charismatic authority in contrast to
mere traditionalism and to the "rationality" of legal
authority. Moreover, whereas Sohm thinks of a "fall" in
the church from charisma into law, Max Weber speaks of

"the routinization of charisma." Weber "radicalizes" the concept of charisma so as to make it apply to political and economic as well as to ecclesiastical structures of authority. For Weber charismatic authority is the dynamic element in history which again and again breaks through the encrustations of traditionalism and of rational, legal bureaucratism. Through Max Weber, Sohm in a certain fashion has exercised a marked influence among the sociologists, many of whom have probably not even heard his name.

Sohm's epic does not confine itself to the themes we have noted above. He traces the recurrent rise and fall of world-fleeing and world-coercing monasticism, at the same time stressing its role in the interiorizing and individualizing of piety; he observes the overemphasis on the subjective aspects of religion in Pietism and Methodism and the overemphasis on objective means of grace in Roman Catholicism; he gives a dramatic account of the struggles between church and state; in accord with his life-long interest as a jurist, he gives attention to the character and significance of voluntary associations; and he stresses the significance of the Enlightenment and of Liberalism in the development of modern Protestantism. In these expositions he frequently oversimplifies. He even ignores wide stretches of church history and of Christian thought. He does not even mention Thomas Aquinas, viewing him perhaps as a precursor of the lamented scholasticism of seventeenth-century Protestantism in Germany; he leaves entirely out of account the Radical Reformation (the Left Wing) to which his own spiritualism bears some affinity; he provides a lopsided view of the Enlightenment and of Liberalism, neglecting the development of modern historical research and of the modern historical consciousness (though he stresses the value of the ideal of freedom in Liberalism and particularly of its "revival of freedom of association") ; and he almost entirely neglects the Anglo-Saxon traditions (Anglican and Nonconformist) and the whole issue of separation of church and state.

Yet, the *Outlines* will be read for years to come. It induces the reader to ask some typically Protestant questions about Christian faith and about the relations between Christianity and culture, and between Christianity and society. In his way of pressing these questions, Sohm can hardly be considered an "objective" historian. He rejected the ideal of the merely "objective" historian as illusory. His purpose was to write an epic of Christian faith in its struggle with worldly powers, for he was convinced that "the world is empty, because heaven is empty first."

JAMES LUTHER ADAMS
Edward Mallinckrodt, Jr. Professor of Divinity
Harvard Divinity School

# DIVISION I

## THE BEGINNING

### INTRODUCTION

### CHAPTER 1

#### PERSECUTION

### CHAPTER II

#### INTERNAL DEVELOPMENT

### CHAPTER III

#### THE CHURCH OF THE EMPIRE

# CONTENTS

# DIVISION II

# THE MIDDLE AGES

# CONTENTS

# DIVISION III

## THE AGE OF THE REFORMATION

### CHAPTER I

#### REFORMATION

### CHAPTER II

#### COUNTER REFORMATION

# DIVISION IV

## PIETISM AND THE ILLUMINATION

# CONTENTS

# DIVISION V

## THE NINETEENTH CENTURY

# Division I

# THE BEGINNING

## INTRODUCTION

### § 1. *The World*

LET us go back to the first century of our era.

In Strasburg the legionary is drawing up his sentinels on guard and the Roman word of command is resounding. The Roman eagle is supreme, not only on the Rhine. but on the Danube, the Euphrates, the Nile, at the foot of the Atlas and of the Pyrenees. With the rise of the empire the full power of the Roman state springs into life. The provinces are flourishing under a wise government. A single will sways the vast army. Along with energetic warfare against the outside enemy, we see peace and prosperity united within the empire. Commerce is flourishing; and the rich culture of the Hellenic East spreads far and wide over the Latin West, bearing life and blessing in its train and raising art and learning to a new development.

A golden age has dawned. The kingdom of Rome has come in all its glory.

What more can mankind want? Are not all earthly and spiritual good things showered on it in profusion? They cannot but now say to the passing moment, 'Stay,

thou art so fair!' And yet with all its wealth and all
its culture the highest good is lacking. The old gods
are dethroned. The temples of Jupiter and of Apollo
still stand, but the faith is gone which once worshipped
them in simplicity. The Olympic heaven is empty
now. Its guests, whose forms the ancient world once
beheld in their fulness of sensuous power and of ideal
beauty, have faded into the dream-pictures of poetic
fancy. The cultured world has turned from the gods
of Homer to Philosophy with her many tongues,
Philosophy whose systems end in the one refrain,
'There are no gods.'

The multitude follow after Isis and Serapis, the gods
who have made their entry into Rome out of Egypt.
They find edification in the juggling arts of Etrurian
soothsayers, in the secret and intoxicating solemnities
of the Mysteries, and in the demoralizing Festivals of
Cybele, the great Mother of the gods.

Not that the heathen world had wholly lost its need
of religion and its ideals of religion on the eve of its
dissolution. On the contrary, in the first and second
centuries of the empire, we see a steadily rising development of the religious spirit, with stages marked
by the noble figures of Seneca and Marcus Aurelius.
Philosophy in divesting the old gods of their splendour was at the same time a guide to the one highest
divinity. Philosophy was a schoolmaster to bring the
pagan to Christ, as was to the Jew the Old Testament
law. Though Stoicism represented the creed of the
majority of educated men, with its exhortations to a
life of stern self-discipline on purely natural grounds,
it was becoming more and more influenced by the
Platonic philosophy; and the Platonic quest of the

ideal world which lies behind the sensible became with the philosophers of the empire more and more a long-ing for the divine, a longing for revelation, a longing for redemption. Side by side with the innumerable local worships of the heathen world, the idea of monotheism arose in all its power, ruling as a spiritual ruler over the world of the Roman Empire. But the monotheism towards which ancient philosophy tended was power-less either to displace polytheism, to win real popularity for itself or to secure what men first of all desired—certainty. To this monotheism no power was given to regenerate an ageing world. Even this philosophy also resulted, not in attainment or secure possession, but in the mere longing after the divine—longing which carried at its heart doubt of the existence of the thing longed for.

The world is empty, because heaven is empty first.

Mankind is full of eagerness to discover the kingdom which is from above. That mighty movement of cul-ture, which in the Roman Empire was borne in a single upward direction by the combined forces of the Latin and Hellenic spirits, now culminates in the creation of the world's Desire, which goes forth to meet the world's Saviour.

## § 2. *Christianity*

Over the wide field of the Roman Empire, a few Christian communities are scattered here and there, as yet unnoticed. The new faith has gone forth from Jerusalem. Already (somewhere about the middle of the first century) it has reached Rome and Alexandria. Between these two extreme points are ranged the churches of Greece, Macedonia, Asia Minor, and Syria, for the most part founded by the Apostle Paul in the fifties. Amongst their various members, as yet few in number, those of the Jewish nationality form a prominent part. Side by side with them are Greek slaves and freedmen. Not many rich, not many learned, but many of the common people : handicraftsmen, soldiers, petty traders, fishermen, publicans—the poor and the despised of this world.

It is upon this little society, destitute as it was of all worldly resources, a vanishing quantity in the tumult of the great cities, that the eye of the historian rests. It contains a power which shall one day overcome the world of the Roman Empire.

Seen from the outside, the Christian community seemed to be only one more newly formed club, like countless other unions of the same sort.

The Roman world of the first century was overspread with religious societies. There was no longer any fixed religion, but there were *religions* in plenty—worships of local deities, divine honours paid to men, together with divers religious customs. There were none, especially among the lower classes of the people, who did not belong to some union of the kind. There was a divinity of each society ; and there was always the divinity of the Emperor actually reigning, which was worshipped in regular monthly meetings. There were secret rites of lustration, like the Christian Baptism. There were common meals, like the Christian *Agapæ* and the Lord's Supper. The members of the societies were even formed into a sort of general brotherhood. In the clubs and brotherhoods, just as with the Christians, all class distinctions were done away with. The slave was equal to the freeman, the freedman to the freeborn. There, at the gatherings and festivals of the unions, the most miserable slave could enjoy for an instant freedom and equality. There the poor man could shake off, at least for the moment, the burden of life. Nay more, these unions had relief funds for the needy who had joined for the sake of union, more particularly funds for providing honourable burial for members of the guild. The idea itself of practical brotherly love does not seem to have been peculiar to the Christian communities. To the mere onlooker the association of the lower classes had only developed a new impulse in them. That impulse might come and go like the rest.

But what a difference! Where are the other countless unions which the great need of the masses once called into being in the Roman Empire? Where are they *now*? The wind of history has swept them away. Long ago, many centuries ago, not a trace of them was left. Of all those religious societies of the Roman Empire only two are living to this day: the Jewish Synagogue and the Christian Church. The Jewish Synagogue endures mainly by the living power of the Jewish nationality. The Christian Church, which rested on no exclusive nationality, endures solely in consequence of the living power of its religion.

> 'The history of the world
> Is the world's judgment.'

No other religion has had power to guide the progress of our culture save Christianity alone. Therefore it is that it has conquered. On its side were neither Roman legions nor ancient learning, but the power of divine truth which is mightier than all the powers of our earthly life.

By virtue of the spirit which is alive within her, the Christian Church in its slow upward growth had power to outlast the great Roman Empire, to join the ancient to the modern world, and to be the educator of the race of men that was to come.

# CHAPTER I

## PERSECUTION

### § 3. *Judaism and Christianity*

THE enemy of the Church from its very birth was
Pharisaic Judaism.

Pharisaism, which had sprung from the heroic struggle
of the Maccabees, represented the regenerate Jewish
world, holding itself separate from all that was pagan
and impure, cumbered with the daily service of legal
righteousness, a service made more and more grievous
by the constant addition of new rules. The mass
of the Jewish people was Pharisaically inclined. In
Pharisaism it found its own innate zeal for the law,
found all the proud self-consciousness of Jewish nationality joined to a burning hatred against the heathen
conqueror, and to wild hopes of the kingdom of Judah
which was to be set up over the world by the Messiah.
And now, in the sharpest contrast to this slavish zeal
for the law, appeared the Christian doctrine of the
freedom of God's children from the law; in contrast to
this image of a Jewish Messiah coming in earthly glory,
the form of the Crucified who called heathens and Jews
without distinction into His heavenly kingdom.

Pharisaism meant the completion, Christianity the
abolition of national Judaism.

So the conflict arose at once. Stephen died a
martyr's death (A.D. 36 or 37) because he taught that

Jesus of Nazareth had come to destroy the worship of
the temple and to abolish the forms of the Mosaic law
(Acts vi. 14). Of the Apostles, James, brother of John,
was beheaded under Herod Agrippa (44); Peter was
imprisoned for a while; James, the brother of the Lord,
was stoned (62). As far as its power reached, Judaism
vented its hatred against Christianity in deeds of
violence. For a while the community at Jerusalem
fled before the enmity of the Pharisees and was
scattered abroad, so that only the Apostles had courage
to remain behind in the city. In Pharisaism the Jewish
people fought against Christianity the more bitterly
because the *moral* forces of national Judaism were
attacked by Christianity. Thus even Saul, one of the
noblest of men, went forth, full of holy enthusiasm, to
defend the law of his fathers against the destroyer.

The effect of Pharisaic persecution was to hasten the
spread of Christianity. Nay more, the persecutor himself might find 'as it were scales' fall suddenly from his
eyes. It was to Saul that Christ revealed Himself—the
risen Christ. He saw Him whom he had persecuted;
and the zealous champion of Judaism and of the law
became the Apostle of the Gentiles, who by powerful
preaching was to make known to the Jew and also to
the Greek the justification which comes not by the law
but by faith.

Yet the conflict of Christianity with Judaism was but
the prelude to a mightier battle upon a vaster stage.

## § 4. *Paganism and Christianity*

Christianity had to deal not only with Judaism but
with the world.

The world was Roman.   The fate of the future had to be decided within the Roman Empire.

The Roman Empire was pagan.   What was the attitude of Paganism towards Christianity?

That was clear from the beginning.   Scarcely was the Christian Church founded, when it was attacked by Paganism.

The burning of Rome (A.D. 64) was laid to the charge of the Christians.   A vast number of the brethren, cruelly put to death, fell victims to the revengeful multitude.   The Apostle Paul, who had been long held in captivity in Rome, was probably numbered amongst those who there sealed their faith with their blood about this time ; and with him, so we may fairly suppose, the Apostle Peter likewise suffered martyrdom.

The flames of the burning of the world's capital, together with those living torches, the bodies of the martyrs flaring in the gardens of the Emperor Nero, lit up the Church's entry into the world's history. Hitherto the Christians had been confused by the populace with the Jews.   Now, for the first time, the distinction became generally recognized—the Christians alone, not the Jews, were charged with the burning of Rome.

In the inquiry which was set on foot, the Christians were declared innocent of incendiarism.   But they were condemned all the same, being found guilty of 'hatred against the whole human race.'   The religion of love appeared to the Romans as a religion of hate, and (which was more wonderful) not altogether wrongly— from their point of view.

The Roman believed that his city and her empire

should endure for ever.   His patriotism consisted in this belief.   But the Christian believed in the destruction of the city, the empire, the globe itself.   He believed that one empire alone was eternal—the empire of Christ, the kingdom of God.   Indeed, the early churches believed that the end of the world was close at hand.   The eyes of the disciples had seen Christ who was risen from the dead.   They were persuaded that even in their lifetime they should see Him come again in His divine glory to destroy the earthly order of things, and to judge the quick and the dead.   They longed for this day with all the desire of the bride for the bridegroom.   They longed for the fall of the kingdom of Rome, that so the kingdom of God might come.   Herein was their treason to their country—in their hatred towards the Roman Empire, and thus towards the 'whole human race.'

Rome, that is Paganism, and Christianity stood face to face.   To the old pagan world, the State represented the highest good.   Moral virtue was identified with the active service of the State.   To live and to die for the commonweal was the whole duty of man.   Therefore in that worship of the Emperor which the Roman world had borrowed from the most ancient customs of the East, Paganism found its last and highest expression. The Roman Emperor was the incarnation of the idea of the State.   The altar raised to him was consecrated to the worship of that which, for Paganism, was the highest moral force, the power of the State.   To the new views which the Christians put forward with reckless determination, the worship not only of idols, but of the Emperor (that is, of the State), was irreconcilable. To the Christian the highest of all things was not the

almighty Cæsar, not the Roman Empire, not the Roman
nation.   To the Christian the Highest was, before all,
*not of this world*, for his longing was fixed upon a better.
With Christianity a new theory of the world came into
history, challenging all other to open combat, a theory
which insisted on the worthlessness of all earthly things
when compared with heavenly things ; which rendered
unto Cæsar the things that are Cæsar's, but at the same
time desired to give unto God the things that are God's.
And this theory of the world made in Christianity its
claim to be the only universally valid one.   While Judaism shut itself in from the outer world, and claimed its
promises, as it guarded its beliefs, for itself alone ; while
the philosophical systems appealed only to the learned,
Christianity claimed from the very first to conquer the
world.   It went out into the highways and market-
places for the very purpose of gaining a decisive influence over those modes of popular thought on which the
commonweal now depended.

For this reason Christianity was dangerous to the
State, in the old pagan sense.   It struck at the very
foundations of the ancient State—that State which, with
its unlimited and illimitable power, claimed to regulate
the whole outer and inner life of man.   Virtue was
attacked, virtue in the ancient sense of love for the
commonweal as for the highest good.   The outrages of
the Emperor Nero, the blind rage of the heathen multitude against Christians transported by 'hatred against
the human race,' were but the instinctive and necessary
expression of the ancient political idea of the State,
which had good reason to feel that its very life was
threatened.

## § 5. *Proceedings against the Christians*

To the Roman citizen the Christian, as such, was the enemy of the State; he was suspected of high treason on account of his opinions, and therefore in the eye of the law guilty of death.

The Christian community maintained itself under the pressure of this penal law during three centuries.

It would, however, be an error to imagine this long period as one of unbroken persecution. On the contrary, the law was only carried out now and then, by fits and starts. Times of persecution alternated with long periods of practical toleration. It follows that the persecutions of the earlier periods were throughout of local and limited character. Where plague, famine, or fire stirred up the masses of the people, or where some violent provincial governor felt himself constrained to vent his passion on the Christians, or where the Christians themselves challenged the multitude to opposition, there a persecution arose, now in one place now in another. Thus the burning of Rome gave the pretext for the persecution of the Christians under Nero, but of the Christians in Rome only. Thus Ignatius, bishop of Antioch, died a martyr's death (about 115), and Polycarp, bishop of Smyrna, sealed his faith with his blood upon the scaffold under Antoninus Pius (about 155). Under Marcus Aurelius (161-180), there fell that bloody persecution in Southern Gaul which claimed countless victims from the Christian Church at Lyons (177). Under Septimius Severus, conversion to Christianity was forbidden by law (202), and persecution raged against the Christians in Egypt and in the Latin province of Africa. But, notwithstanding,

up to the middle of the third century there is no
question of a general persecution carried on against the *not general*
Christians in all parts.  In the wide circle of the Roman
Empire the Church had room enough for development,
notwithstanding the conflicts more or less severe by
which particular communities were shaken.

Nevertheless the principle held good that to be a
Christian was to be dedicated to death.  The mere
fact of his Christianity sufficed to found a penal charge
against any member of the community.  The principle
remained, even where it was only imperfectly carried
out.  Not only to the heathen priest or dealer in idols
who were injured in their trades, but to the greedy
provincial governor, to the envious neighbour, to the
revengeful enemy it furnished the long-wished pretext
for bringing the chosen victim to his death, ostensibly
on the ground of his Christianity.  Justin Martyr, a
philosopher who became a Christian, was beheaded in
Rome at the instigation of a rival author, Crescens, who
in this manner vented his literary spite on his enemy.
The number of the martyrs is greater than history has
taken account of.  In the case of Justin, that which
more than all moved him to become a convert to
Christianity was the courage, stronger than death,
wherewith the followers of the Christian faith died for
their opinions.  To the heathen death was the thing of
all others most to be feared ; to the Christian death
was gain.  The moral power of Christianity was
revealed to the heathen world before all in that heroic
courage in dying, a courage which met death not with
contempt, nor yet with stoical indifference, but with the
sure and certain hope of victory.  This was the faith
that in its certain possession of heaven was mighty to

overcome earth.    Faith was the single force which
Christianity opposed to enmity and onslaught, but it
was a force which was strongest and most triumphant
against the enemy where apparently overcome.    Proceedings against the Christians were first definitely
organized under Trajan (112).    The Christians were to
be persecuted and condemned, not officially, but only
on a special charge.    This remained law until far into
the third century.    Even after a rescript of Marcus
Aurelius in 176 or 177, official prosecutions were only
allowed when the Christian religion gave rise to open
disquiet.    But there was a further meaning in the
indulgence of Trajan.    If the accused Christian offered
incense to the image of the Emperor, he went free ; if
he did not offer incense, he lay under sentence of death.
Behind the seeming tenderness lurked a calculating
cruelty.    By the very act of sacrificing to the imperial
image the Christian renounced his Christianity and
escaped sentence of death.    The temptation was terrible,
and many fell victims to it.    Pliny, governor of
Bithynia and Pontus, whose question had given
occasion to this edict of Trajan, was persuaded that it
would soon make an end of Christianity.    If a Christian
refused to sacrifice he was guilty of death, not nominally
for his Christianity, nor for his behaviour before the
accusation, but for the crime of *majestas* or treason
which he had committed by refusing to sacrifice *after*
the accusation.    The prosecution of Christians differed
from all other criminal actions in this : that its one
object was to render the accused person guilty—
through the refusal of the sacrifice required of him.    It
was a refinement of cruelty.    The accused Christian, as
such, was held *suspected* of *majestas*, legal proceedings

being so ordered that if he remained true to his
Christianity he was bound to become guilty. In point
of fact, what the State persecuted was not a *deed*, a
crime already committed, but a *thought*—the Faith of
Christianity, the Faith that refused to worship any
earthly thing, even if it were the Roman State. The
proceedings against the Christians, in the form in which
they were instituted by Trajan, made it indubitably
clear, that the pagan state, with its claim to be the
supreme moral exemplar, had declared war against
Christianity.

## § 6. *The Decisive Battle*

But the Church grew and never ceased growing.
Already in the second half of the second century
Christianity played a strikingly conspicuous part in the
life of the people. About the middle of the third
century Paganism discovered that its very existence
was threatened. The Christian community in Rome,
which was certainly the largest of the Christian communities, must have numbered at this time at least
twenty thousand members. Through its ecclesiastical
constitution, which in the meanwhile had matured, it
had even become a social power apparently equal to
the State. If Rome was to preserve that national and
political character which had been transmitted to her
of old, now was the moment for interference.

From this date (the middle of the third century) the
pagan state began its systematic persecution of the
Christians, over the whole extent of the empire, and
formed against the Church an organized plan of attack
which it carried out with all the means in its power.

The attack was begun by the Emperor Decius (249-251). He gave orders for a *general* persecution of the Christians. The authorities all over the empire were to interfere against the whole body of the Christians, officially, that is, without waiting for any special charge against them, and compel them to sacrifice. A fearful time followed, which claimed countless martyrs. Even the death of Decius brought only temporary relief. Under his successor Gallus (251-253), after two years of peace, fresh edicts were issued against the Christians in 253. But it was Valerian (253-260) who, more than all, took up the work of Decius after the year 257. In 258 he commanded that all bishops, priests, and deacons of the Church, together with all Christian senators and judges, should be condemned to death, if they refused to recant. By this time there was method in the attack. It aimed at destroying, not, as under Decius, the whole body of the Christians (this had at length proved impracticable), but the organization of the Church, together with every one of the higher ranks who belonged to it. The formless undisciplined masses that remained would, it was hoped, be powerless to uphold Christianity. In Carthage the bishop Cyprian, in Rome the deacon Laurentius (St. Laurentius of the Catholic Church), and with them many others, fell victims to this persecution. But the repeal of the edicts of persecution (260-261) was one of the first measures passed by Gallienus, who, after the death of his father Valerian, reigned as sole Emperor from the year 260. Not that the Christian religion met with just recognition and tolerance from him. Under him also and his successors the profession of the Christian faith remained punishable by death; and the law might be put into execution any instant, so soon as the refusal to offer incense to the imperial image (on the part of a Christian soldier, for instance) had been legally proved. But the order was repealed by which magistrates were compelled to search out all followers of the Christian faith and prove every such refusal by means of a legal prosecution. A state of practical toleration existed in which the law was only carried out in isolated instances. There followed an interval of peace which lasted forty years. It was the stillness before the storm. Under Diocletian (284-305) the Roman kingdom rose up once more against the hated enemy, in order to re-establish the absolute monarchy of the State in all its former glory. It was the bitterest persecution which the Church had yet seen. It was a battle for life or death.

Towards the end of his reign, after having left the Christians in peace for seventeen years, Diocletian was urged to this attack upon the Church by his son-in-law, the Cæsar Galerius, a brave, stern, but uneducated soldier, who cherished a fanatical hatred against the Christians.

Nicomedia was the imperial residence. The destruction of the Church at Nicomedia (on the 23rd of February 303) gave the signal for the attack. The next day the imperial edict was published. All Christian officers were to retire from the army, and all Christian officials from their posts. All Christian churches were to be destroyed, all the sacred books of the Christians confiscated and burned. It was instantly followed by a second edict commanding all clergy to be put in prison, in order to compel them to sacrifice. A

third edict, issued in the year 304, commanded all
Christians to sacrifice, and that under penalty of
death. The most comprehensive measures were taken
in order to enforce the execution of this law. But
this was hardly possible. Smitten by an incurable
disease, Diocletian resigned the imperial crown (305).
Galerius, chief Augustus of the empire from the year
306, now pursued his own course unhindered in his
Eastern Empire. From this moment there began in
the East the first really bloody persecution of the
Christians, a persecution no longer checked by any
reasonable scruple. It was an insane butchery. The
Christians were to be compelled to sacrifice by fair
means or foul. The food exposed for sale in the
market-places was even drenched with sacrificial wine,
in order that the Christians might be made sacrificers
in this way. A tremendous tumult went through the
length and breadth of the empire. Even actual
resistance was made in some places. After four long,
melancholy, fearful years (306-310), Galerius, in sore
sickness, recognized that he must draw back. On the
30th of April, while lying on his death-bed, he issued
an edict of general toleration. He had to confess that
the Christians had conquered. The work thus begun
was ended by Constantine, the son of the tolerant
Constantius Chlorus (who ruled as Cæsar in the West).
Fighting under the Sign of the Cross, he first wrested
Italy from the usurper Maxentius, and then issued his
famous edicts of toleration, published in Rome, 312,
for his own West-Roman Empire, and again in Milan,
313, for the entire empire, in concert with his fellow-
Emperor, Licinius. Christianity was placed upon the
same level as Paganism. Every man was at liberty to

'choose his own divinity and to worship whom 'he would.' Freedom of worship was granted to the Christians all over the Roman Empire. The grievous time was over, and the Church breathed again. Upon the dark night had followed the clear, full light of day.

## § 7. *The Church and Her Victory*

To what was the victory of Christianity owing? Was it to the steadfastness, to the heroic courage, of its adherents? By no means. As it had been already in the time of the governor Pliny, in the beginning of the second century, even so in the time of the Decian persecution, and, if possible, still more under that of Diocletian, the number of Christians who fell away from their faith was enormous. It would give a false picture to represent the body of the Christians, in the first three centuries, after the type of those martyrs whose memory the Church has rightly glorified. The mass of the Christians then, as at all times, were cowardly, wavering in their faith, feeble in their profession before men, and incapable of resistance in the hour of danger. When persecution came, too many were ready to forswear their faith, in order to save property, position, and life. The community had already become large. As its numbers rose its inner force declined. The Church no longer looked for the end of the world as close at hand. She took her place in the world, not without absorbing something of the world's spirit. She flung her doors wide open, and along with the inthronging masses of the people, all that was weak and ignoble in human nature made its entrance unhindered into the Christian community. Obviously the relations amongst her members in the early age of the Church, where a narrow circle of believers clung to each other like brethren would be other than they were in later times when about one-half of the city had embraced Christianity. Practical brotherly love disappeared, or the exercise of it was left to the clergy as representing the community. Church discipline became even more lax and indulgent as regarded lay members. Two codes of morality appeared: one for the clergy, from whom the full energy of a Christian life was exacted; and another for the laity, for whom it was fairly sufficient if they refrained from grosser transgressions. Already, from the middle of the second century, we see the secularization of the Church making unbroken progress. Nevertheless, this state of things was inevitable if the Church was to fulfil her high calling, to win the world over to herself. The world received of the spirit of Christianity, but Christianity no less received of the spirit of the world. When we consider the great mass of believers in the third century, even many of the best of them—the martyr Cyprian for instance, whom the Catholic Church rightly honours among her Saints—in spite of the powerful personality of some true bishops of the fold, we find many who are Christians only in name, and much, far too much, hatred and enmity, envy, ambition, and worldly covetousness. Already about the middle of the second century a Roman Christian saw in the spirit the vision of a Church covered with wrinkles and spots, and full of all manner of diseases. Even so was it in reality. The spirit of the first martyrs had perished, and the Roman State of Decius and Diocletian saw opposed to it a Church already grown old, a Church secularized and

fallen from her ideal, when it prepared to wage a war of
extermination against Christianity. Hence the many
apostasies, hence the fearful devastation which the last
great persecutions brought upon the Church.

And yet the Church has remained unconquerable.
The marvel of Christianity and its greatest achievement *Marvel*
is just this: that it could not be destroyed, that it won
the victory although so miserably represented by its
followers. Apostasy, weaknesses, and sin have had no
power to destroy the imperishable strength of Christianity. It became secularized, yet it still remained
a leaven to leaven the whole world. It was betrayed
by the greater number of its followers, yet there abode
within it that spirit, which, in one little band of the
chosen, in spite of sin and error, was powerful enough
to overcome the world, and, through its glorious example
of martyrdom, to arouse the spirit of resistance even in
the ranks of the lukewarm, the wavering, and the faint.
By this time Christianity was no more that unknown
religion against which the falsest and most hideous
scandals were circulated and believed (as in the first and
second centuries). The spirit of Christianity had become *visible*, and it stretched forth its sheltering wing
over its followers. Throughout the length and breadth
of the heathen world a yearning for Monotheism, which
had arisen in all its power from the ruins of the ancient
worships, went forth to meet the true God of the
Christians. When in the third century the State
declared war against the Church, it found the people's
old tempestuous hatred against Christianity no longer
on its side. Numbers of Christians had received
welcome and protection in heathen homes; and in the
West practically no attempt was made to carry out the

edicts of persecution issued by Diocletian and Galerius.
Already, not only were the convictions of the best minds
of the age opposed to the State, but it had against it
the whole of the spiritual power wherewith Christianity
(once seen as it truly is) influences even the outer world.
That spiritual power was made manifest and developed
all its forces to the utmost, in spite of the weakness of
its followers.

Through all the shades and darkness which surround
us in the history of the Christian Church, there breaks
forth evermore victorious—like the sun going forth in
his strength, rending the clouds asunder and gleaming
through the rift now in one place, now in another—the
imperishable light of true Christianity.

So it was even then. The Church conquered, not
because of the Christians, but in spite of them—through
the power of the Gospel.

# CHAPTER II

## INTERNAL DEVELOPMENT

### § 8. *Jewish Christianity*

THE persecution which attacked her from without was
the least danger which the Church had to fear. Far
more fatal was it that the self-same powers with which
Christianity had to battle had found their way into the
very heart of the community, where their aim was to
destroy the true character of the Christian Creed and
thereby to sap the forces of its life.

First came Pharisaism, then Paganism.

In the young community Pharisaic influences soon
made themselves felt. Not all Pharisees, on their
conversion to Christianity, underwent that process of
inner development which so completely changed the
Apostle Paul. Thus a Pharisaic tendency (so-called
Jewish Christianity) appeared in the Church, the aim
of which was to Judaize Christianity. The Pharisaic
Christians believed that the crucified Jesus was the
Messiah, but they maintained that salvation through
Christ was only for the Jews. He who would be a
Christian, according to their doctrine, must first become
a Jew, by circumcision, and take upon him the burden
of the whole Jewish law. This sort of Christianity was
only a new form of Judaism. Out of a religion for the
world had again arisen a religion for a nation.

Jewish Christianity was in open contradiction with

the words of the Lord, who called the heathen as well
as the Jews to be direct partakers of His kingdom.[1]
As openly did it contradict the Christianity of the
primitive community. Why was the persecuting hatred
of the Pharisees aroused against the primitive Church,
if not because the Christianity of that Church proclaimed
the dissolution of the service of the Temple, and the
transformation of the Mosaic law (Acts vi. 14)? What
else but zeal for the 'traditions of his fathers' kindled
Saul's righteous indignation against the Christians (Gal.
i. 14)? And what of the great Gentile Christian Church
of Antioch, which had received Christianity without the
rite of circumcision and without the Jewish law (Acts
xi. 20; xv. 1)?

Gentile Christianity was by no means created first
of all by the Apostle Paul. He defended the Gentile
Christianity which was already there before him, and
for which he was the first to open out a new and wider
way. His quarrel was not with the older apostles, they
gave to him rather 'the right hands of fellowship' (Gal.
ii. 9), but with the 'false brethren,' who were 'unawares
brought in,' who 'came in privily,' and thus represented
a younger element in the Church (Gal. ii. 4). As the
water of a river takes its colour from the bed over which
it flows, so Christianity was involuntarily coloured by
those nationalities which, in its missionary activity, it
absorbed. The first nationality upon which Christianity
acted, and from which indeed it had arisen, was the
Jewish people. It was inevitable that the Jewish people
should in its turn influence Christianity. Out of these
influences, already indicating a transformation of primitive Christianity, arose this narrow - minded Jewish

[1] See, for instance, Matt. xxi. 43; Luke xiii. 29, 30, etc.

Christianity. It was powerful enough to cause even the
older apostles to waver. It was supported by all the
natural instincts of national Judaism. Yet the apostles,
Peter and John, even James, the Lord's brother, so
stern in his attachment to the law, gave to the Apostle
Paul the right hand of fellowship, in recognition of the
Gospel which he had preached to the Gentiles without
laying upon them the burden of the law. Opinions
differed as to the question whether the Jewish law was
binding on the converted Jew, after, as before his conversion. James answered the question in the affirmative,
while the Apostle Peter wavered, at least for a time
(Gal. ii. 11, 12). The negative decision was implied in
the very essence of primitive Christianity, and for this
reason it won the victory in the Church. By that right N
hand of fellowship an agreement was made between the
Apostle Paul and the older apostles : he was to preach
the gospel to the Gentiles, they to the Jews (Gal. ii. 9).
This division of their fields of mission pointed to a
difference in their convictions respecting the precise
value of the Jewish law for the Jewish Christian world.
All the same, this opposition of the leaders can have
been no lasting one. We hear nothing of the division
of their fields of mission in the subsequent history of the
Church. On the contrary, it is probable that Peter may
have also laboured in Rome, as did Paul, and he appears
to have had dealings even with the Corinthian Church,
which was of purely Pauline origin (1 Cor. i. 12) ; while,
on the other hand, John stood in close relations with
the Pauline Churches of Asia Minor, especially in
Ephesus (Rev. ii. 3). In spite of all sorts of differences,
which in the Corinthian Church, for instance, gave rise
to no less than four parties even in the lifetime of Paul

(1 Cor. i. 12), from the very first we see one united movement, like a mighty stream, flowing through the Churches. From the end of the first century onward, so soon as we can recognize in the evidence of tradition the life, not merely of single prominent personages, but of entire communities, we see before us in full swing, dominating the whole Church, a Christianity free from the fetters of the Jewish law, a Christianity which, in spite of this freedom, bears nowhere the characteristic traits of an exact Pauline Christianity ; a certain proof that it could not have been founded by Paul individually. The accidental circumstance, that the epistles of Paul chiefly have been handed down to us from the very earliest times, has easily given rise to the error of over-rating the importance of those special differences against which he had to fight.

The history of the Church shows that from the first the ruling power in Christianity has been neither Jewish Christianity, nor even Gentile Christianity of exclusively Pauline type. These were the opposite extremes that sprang up side by side within the Church. The Apostle Paul laboured powerfully as a tool in the hands of God. Nevertheless, our Christianity, our deliverance from the slavish service of the law, before all else the triumphant claim of that Christianity to be the religion of the world (that for all nations it might change their relation to God from bondage into son-ship), we owe, not to him, not to the Apostle, but to a greater than he—to our Lord Christ, the Son of Man, who is at the same time the Son of God.

## § 9. *Gentile Christianity*

Christianity went forth from Palestine to conquer the world of Greece and Rome. As in the primitive age the influence of national Judaism was mainly felt in the Church, so in the succeeding epoch it was inevitable that pagan thought should assert itself as a living power. In the second century Christianity spread far and wide over pagan lands. Hence the powerful rise of Gnos- *γγ* ticism, which displays the influence of Paganism on Christianity as of Christianity on Paganism.

Pagan religion arose out of the primeval worship of Nature. Heaven and earth, with all the forces they hold within them, were transformed in the poetic imagination of the nations into living forms of the gods wherein humanity could henceforth worship both Nature and its own Ideal. Yet Paganism never lost the remembrance of its origin. It preserved that remembrance in the Mysteries. Here, in the circle of the *μ* initiated, was guarded the memory of that ancient holy worship of the powers of Nature, sombre or joyous; while faith in the more approachable human gods was left to the multitude. Here, too, were preserved many of those profounder ethical conceptions which in the popular religion found only symbolical expression. Compared with the wisdom of the Mysteries, the popular religion was mere allegory. The initiated beheld Truth herself unveiled, the multitude saw but the hem of her garment. From the pagan world Mysticism made its way into Christianity in the beginning of the second century. This was the origin of Gnosticism. Gnosis (γνῶσις) means knowledge. Gnosticism promised to its followers in the form of knowledge that which in Christianity was living Truth. It sought the secret, the mystery which was hidden in Christianity as in the popular pagan religion. This conception of Truth did away with the difference between Christianity and the various forms of pagan worship. In Christianity, as well as Paganism, truth must lie behind the facts with which ordinary faith was satisfied. This truth had been unduly displaced by dim recollections of a primitive worship of Nature, by pagan mythology and the dogmas of the Christian creed, and was to be given back to the Gnostic by his philosophy.

The key-note which runs through the chief Gnostic systems is the philosophical idea of the antithesis between spirit and matter, and the conception, borrowed from the old pagan Nature-worship, of the opposition between light and darkness. God is the God of Light who from the depths of His own being brings forth a series of spirits of light (Æons), in a descending order. Opposed to him stands Matter, or Chaos, with the inferior spirits of darkness. The world was created out of matter by one of those inferior spirits, the Demiurge (δημιουργός), a being not divine. Hence its imperfections, and hence the evil whose source is matter. Gnosticism was an anticipation of modern pessimism ; this world was created the worst of all possible worlds. But Christ is the Æon of Light, who, by taking unto Himself matter, overcomes the kingdom of darkness. In Gnosticism we see the philosophy of the Roman Empire, with its monotheistic tendency, making its first great practical effort to win over the world of its own time. It gives eloquent expression to the need of the educated classes for both revelation and redemption, and to their longing for a Supreme God. It shows at the same time the high position which Christianity from the beginning of the second century had won in the spiritual life of the Roman Empire. These Gnostic philosophers gave the first place to Christianity in order that, with the help of the facts of salvation believed, proclaimed, and defended by the Christian Church, they might gain that which they above all desired—the certainty that God is, and that, above this earthly kingdom with its imperfections, a higher kingdom has arisen, full of life and blessedness, which the spiritual man (ὁ πνευματικός) can gain, if, by means of knowledge (γνῶσις), he has freed himself from the dark powers of matter. But to the Gnostic the Christian creed was only a means of winning a stronger assurance of the truth of his philosophical creed. To this end the historical facts upon which Christianity rests must be taken in an allegorical sense, and, from the moment in which the history is treated as a mere symbol, the persuasive power which lies in the facts as such will be lost beyond recall. Gnosticism remained philosophy, even when it attached itself to Christianity, and therefore shared the inevitable fate of all philosophy, to end, in spite of all its pretensions, in doubt and uncertainty.

Thus, in a certain sense, Gnosticism was the Rationalism of the second century. It substituted for Christianity a philosophical religion, supposed to be more enlightening to the reason, a religion founded on a supposed knowledge of the relations and forces of the universe, but in reality based on the traditions of the heathen world, on ideas borrowed from ancient philosophy, and on the old pagan worship of heaven and earth. The god of the Gnostics is 'the Abyss,' 'the

Silence,' 'the Non-existent,' 'the Incomprehensible,' 'the Unapproachable.' The living God of Christianity is transformed again into the unknown god of the philosophers and of the Mysteries.

The Church saw that here was a power that, in spite of its friendly attitude towards Christianity, was at heart its most determined foe.

The Church was conscious that her power lay in this: that her faith was *not* Philosophy, that its subject-matter could *not* be turned into intellectual conceptions and theories, and that the upright life which reveals the individual Christian as the true 'philosopher' rested *not* upon knowledge of philosophical ideas, but upon *experience* of the Divine Love actually and truly revealed in Christ.

In Gnosticism Philosophy stood opposed to the Church, and that as the mightiest power in the ancient world.

We shall well understand the danger which threatened the Church from this side when we consider further that Gnosticism attracted the vulgar herd by its mysterious rites and ceremonies, that it took possession of the whole pagan world by the charm of a mysticism handed down from an ancient past, by its claim to satisfy at once the mind and the heart, and by its harmony with traditional ways of thinking; while at the same time it satisfied the higher order of minds by the stern morality upheld in most of the Gnostic systems. The whole of the second, and even of the third century is taken up by the battle of the Church with Gnosticism. It was a battle fought to deliver the simple truth of those saving facts which the Church believed from the results of allegorizing pagan speculation. Gnosticism was the treaty of peace which the culture of the second century offered to Christianity. Had Christianity agreed to the terms it would have perished together with that culture. The Church had to be guarded from this treaty of peace.

The Church conquered in the hard-fought fight. We see the full meaning of the conflict in the results which it has had for her. Through this battle with Gnosticism the Canon of the New Testament Scriptures was finally fixed, *i.e.* the number of those books which the Church recognized as authoritative witnesses to Christian truth, as opposed to the erroneous doctrines of the Gnostics. Through this battle Christian theology, and with it the ecclesiastical constitution of the future, received its form. The Church maintained herself not only against the pagan State, but against pagan philosophy and mysticism—far more dangerous foes. But she did not come forth out of this conflict unchanged. In defending itself against Gnosticism the Christianity of the primitive age was transformed into the Catholicism of the next.

## § 10. *Constitution of the Church. Catholicism*

From the unity of all believers in Christ as a single great society comes the development of the Church and of her constitution. We call this assembly of all Christians the *Church*. In primitive times it was called the *ecclesia*, that is to say, the people of God. Christendom is the true Israel, God's chosen people of the new covenant. To this people of God has been promised the presence of Christ, and therefore of God, in the midst of it. In the *ecclesia* every individual

Christian enjoys perfect communion with God through Christ, together with the fulness of all divine and spiritual gifts of grace. The Christian must be a member of Christendom, of the *ecclesia*, of the Church. Hence the question : *Where* is the *ecclesia*?

The apostolic age answered the question thus :—

Where two or three are gathered together in Christ's name, there is the *ecclesia*, the Church. For Christ has said, 'Where two or three are gathered together in My name, *there am I in the midst of them*' (Matt. xviii. 20). The Lord is risen indeed! He is alive for evermore! That is the victorious creed of Christendom. The Lord is in the midst of them who believe on Him, in His divine omnipresence, He that is, and was, and is to come, the Almighty. Therefore He is and works everywhere wheresoever two or three are gathered together in His name. Where Christ is, there is the Church. The Church appears and works in *every* congregation of believers. Even where only two or three are gathered together in His name, there is Christ the Lord in the midst of them, and therefore all Christendom is gathered together with them, working with all its gifts of grace. *There is no need of any human priesthood.* There, in every congregation of believers, is the true Baptism and the true Lord's Supper, the full communion with Christ the High Priest and Mediator of all who believe on Him. *Still less is there any need of a legal constitution.* In fact, every form of legal constitution is excluded.

It is by no means essential to the Church, to Christendom, that it should have a legal constitution, with Pope and Bishops, Superior Ecclesiastical Council,

and Superintendents, after the fashion of the State. On
the contrary, if every congregation of believers represents the Church, that is, the whole of Christendom
with Christ its head, then no single congregation has
any legal authority over another. And if Christ alone
is the head of Christendom, that is, of the Church
which is Christ's body, then no man may presume to
make himself the head of the Church. 'The princes of
this world exercise dominion and authority; but it
shall not be so among you' (Matt. xx. 26). God, that
is, Christ, rules and binds together all the members
of Christendom solely through the gifts of grace
(χαρίσματα) given by Him. To one is given the gift
of teaching, to another the gift of interpretation, to a
third the gift of comfort. The gift of teaching is at the
same time the gift of government. God's people, the
*ecclesia*, is to be ruled, not by man's word, but by the
Word of God proclaimed by the divinely gifted teacher;
and the *ecclesia* obeys the word of the teacher only if,
and so far as, it recognizes therein the Word of God.
Thus the Apostles built up and guided Christendom
through the Word. Besides the Apostles, others, called
prophets and teachers, were stirred up by God in
Christendom, as mighty in the Word (1 Cor. xii. 28).
The Apostles exercised no papal authority. Their
power was the Word of God alone, which the community obeyed because it recognized that Word as the
Word of God. It was just the same with the prophets
and teachers; their government was purely spiritual;
in point of fact they ruled, but without legal authority.
How could their word be made the Word of God by
any legal authority? Apostles, prophets, and teachers
were by no means the only ministers to whom the

preaching of the Word was committed. 'When ye come together,' writes the Apostle Paul, 'every one of you hath a psalm, hath a doctrine, hath a tongue, hath a revelation, hath an interpretation' (I Cor. xiv. 26). In every one after his kind the Word of God is alive to the edifying of the Church, even if the special gifts of the apostle, prophet, or teacher be not given to him. Therefore the Word of God is alive in every congregation of believers. The Church has no absolute need of any class of officials. They are all born ministers of the Word—and ministers they ought to be. They all, by the Holy Spirit living within them, are bearers of the keys of heaven, and of the royal power which in the House of God is given to the Word of God. They are all *priests* and *kings* (Rev. i. 6).

How is it possible under these conditions even to imagine a *legal* government of the Church—of God's people? or any one *legal* priesthood or kingship which could take from another its priestly and kingly power? The Church, the people of God, signifies a *spiritual* people ; the kingdom which is established in the Church is a *spiritual* kingdom ; Christendom forms not a state nor a political union, but is a *spiritual* power. Once for all, a legally constituted Church cannot be.

And yet there has arisen such a thing as Church law. How was that possible?

The reason is not far to seek : Because the natural man is a born enemy of Christianity. There is in our nature a longing for salvation through Christ, the Immanuel, the Prince of Peace ; and yet we strive against Him. Our heart opens itself to every word of Him who is the sunshine of the soul, and yet it sets itself against complete surrender, in its despair, its

misery, and weariness of the world.   The *natural* man
desires to remain under law.   He strives against the
freedom of the Gospel, and he longs with all his strength
for a religion of law and statute.   He longs for some
legally appointed service, in the performance of which
he may exhaust his duty towards God, and so for the
rest of his time be free for the service of the world, free
from that 'reasonable service,' the presenting of his
whole life as a sacrifice to God.   He longs for a legally
appointed Church, for a kingdom of Christ which may
be seen with the eyes of the natural man, for a temple
of God, built with earthly gold and precious stones, that
shall take the heart captive through outward sanctities,
traditional ceremonies, gorgeous vestments, and a ritual
that tunes the soul to the right pitch of devotion.
Before all, he longs for an impressive, authoritative
constitution, one that shall overpower the senses, and
rule the world, a wonderful constitution whose fabric
shall rise upward and reach outward far and wide.   He
desires, as the key-stone of the whole, a fixed body of
doctrine that shall give certain intelligence concerning
all divine mysteries, presented to him in a literal form,
giving an answer to every possible question.   Christ
walked on the sea : man would do so likewise.   Alas,
he sinks !   He desires a rock which his eyes can see—
the visible Church, the visible Word of God.   Everything must be made visible, so that he may grasp it.
From these impulses of the natural man, born at once
of his longing for the gospel and his despair of attaining
to it, Catholicism has arisen.   Herein lies the secret of
the enormous power it has had over the masses who
are 'babes ;' it satisfies these cravings.   *The natural*
*man is a born Catholic.*   We are but servants of God

by natural generation: sonship is first given us by regeneration.

Church law has arisen from this overpowering desire of the natural man for a legally constituted, *catholicized* Church. The development which was to result in the world-ruling power of the Papacy and in the secularization of the Church of Christ, originated, strangely enough, in the celebration of the Eucharist, the Lord's Supper. The meeting of believers at the Eucharist was the only one which made definite outward forms necessary. Its forms determined not only the architecture of our churches but the growth of their constitution.

In the Lord's Supper is repeated Christ's last supper with His disciples. A single person had, in the place of Christ, to break the bread, to bless the wine, and to give thanks, that is to say, to lead the congregation. He was the president of the Eucharistic meeting. Further, as soon as the gathering became so great that all could not sit together at the supper-table, the place at God's table (the altar) was reserved for the persons of highest honour in the community. They thus became fellow-presidents of the meeting. Further, helpers were required to serve, to carry the consecrated elements to those members of the meeting who sat or stood in the body of the room.

The president was called the bishop (literally overseer, shepherd), the fellow-presidents the clergy (literally, the society, the people of God, that is, the Church's select representatives at the supper-table); they who served were called deacons (literally, servants) of the Eucharistic meeting. As clergy, that is, as the select representatives of the Church, the elders or presbyters,

that is, those older members of the community who
were already proved by a life of Christian purity and
charity, sat in a half-circle around the bishop at the
supper-table.   Thus: first the bishop, after him the
presbyters, the deacons, and the people.  Not that this
order was by any means made matter of law.  No one
had a right to the office of bishop; no one a right to
the seat of honour; no one a right to serve as a deacon.
In every single case, it lay properly with the congregation to decide whom it should appoint to these posts.
The office of bishop, as that of the administrator of the
Word, belonged properly to one who had received the
gift of teaching : an apostle, a prophet, or teacher.  But
such teachers, in the apostolic sense, were rare in the
Christian community; so that as a rule the office of
bishop was committed to one of the elders.  It changed
from hand to hand.   It follows that, in the early
Church, *several* elders were commonly appointed, that
is, elected; and then, in each case, the administration
of the bishops on behalf of the congregation was
committed to one of them.  Thus, there was not *one*
bishop, but in every community that was at all
organized, there were several bishops appointed together (see, for instance, Phil. i. 1), a proof that none
had any right to the office of bishop to the exclusion
of another.

To develop the legal constitution of the Church
from this order of the Eucharistic meeting, but one
step was needed : to change the many episcopates into
a single monarchical episcopate, with one bishop as
its head.   Thereby exclusive right to the office of
bishop came to be given to this individual.   This
happened in the beginning of the second century.

Belief in the free exercise of grace declined. The larger the assembly became, the more was felt the need of some fixed outward order. The natural man desires some legal surety that the Word and the Sacraments are administered to him aright. He desires the full establishment of the Church as a kingdom which is of this world. It follows that the community had not seldom to be guarded against robbery by swindlers who went about in the guise of 'prophets,' and knew well how to excite the ready charity of the brethren. Election by the community now received a legal meaning and importance. Only *one* person was to be elected, whose legal office it was to administer the Eucharist and settle the affairs of the Church. This one henceforth received the name of bishop in a special sense. He was now *the* bishop of the Church, the guardian of souls, the teacher, the preacher above all the others. Now, for the first time, in the second century, there was one constitutional Bishop of Rome, one Bishop of Corinth, etc. The Church received a certain legal constitutional form. The elders (presbyters) of the Church were made subordinate to the one bishop elected by the community.

Now the most important thing is this: this single bishop, as one called by God through the common voice of the people, has now alone the right to act as the organ of the *ecclesia*, and is henceforth regarded as indispensable to its life and action. To him, in the first place, belongs the power of speaking at ecclesiastical meetings, as well as the right to administer Baptism and the Lord's Supper, and only by his permission is this power and right accorded to another. Without the bishop, or his appointed representative, there can be no celebration of the Lord's Supper, no consecration or ordination of clergy, nor any business undertaken for which the authoritative sanction of the *ecclesia* (Christendom, the Church) is necessary. *Where the bishop is, there alone is the ecclesia.* The bishop alone has full power to administer the affairs of the Church. Universal priesthood, in the apostolic sense, has disappeared. Under the bishop are the presbyters as his helpers and representatives. Thus the presbyters have some share, if only a limited one, in the priestly character belonging to the bishop. The special priesthood of a sacerdotal class (the bishop and presbyters) has taken the place of the general priesthood of all believers.

The Church (*ecclesia*) is now no longer represented in every assembly of believers, but only in those assemblies presided over by bishop and presbyters. Christ is no longer everywhere, wheresoever two or three are gathered together in His name, He is only there where the bishop and presbyters are. In order to have full communion with Christ, in order to receive worthily the sacraments of Baptism and the Lord's Supper, the Christian now stands in need of *communion with the bishop and the order of presbyters*.

The Church has changed, not merely her constitution, but her faith. Personal communion with Christ is the secret and the power of her Christian life. This communion with Christ and with God is now dependent on outward forms and conditions. This is the essence of Catholicism. Dependence on an outward organism, represented by bishop and presbyters, is the new law which has become binding on every Christian. The *ecclesia*, the Church, the people of God, will only be found there where the Church's officials, the bishop and presbyters, appear. The Church is no longer founded on the communion of believers, as such, but upon the *office*, which is henceforth indispensable to the relations of the Church with Christ. Christendom, the body of Christ, the *ecclesia*, has henceforth a definite, legal constitution—the episcopal ; and he who would belong to Christ must belong to this legal and visible Church (*extra ecclesiam nulla salus !*). The idea of a Catholic Church appears, which is the foundation of all Catholicism.

This astonishing transformation was completed in the Church's battle with false doctrine. The Gnostics, on their side, claimed to have proclaimed to the Church the truth as it is. Where was the authoritative power that could avenge the real truth against false doctrine ? The Canon of the New Testament was still fluctuating ; Christian theology was yet in process of formation. The only power that could victoriously combat Gnosticism was the living tradition of the Church. But where was the true Church ? The Gnostics also claimed to be the true Church. The only resource was to fall back upon the ecclesiastical office. Where the legitimate ecclesiastical official, namely, the bishop, represents beyond all doubt an unbroken connection with the earliest times, there, and there alone (so it appeared), is the Church, and there alone her true tradition. The bishop (so it was now believed) is the successor of the Apostles. The first bishop of a church received both office and doctrine direct from the Apostles, the second bishop from the first, and so on. Where the bishop is, there is the Church and her genuine apostolic tradition.

Gnostic heresy was overcome neither by logical proof nor theological learning, but by means of the natural regard which came to be paid to the ecclesiastical office. The bishop was now the single person whose gifts of grace and that which they implied (namely, the divine call to the ministry of the Word, by the Church's election) were formally recognized and established beyond doubt. The free ministry of the old order, which in Gnosticism had proved serviceable to the spread of false doctrine, was triumphantly displaced by the formal and exclusive ministry of the bishop recognized by the Church. It was as the teacher provided by God, after the manner of an apostle, with the divine gift of knowledge (*charisma veritatis*, as Irenæus calls it, writing about 180) that the bishop was victorious over Gnostic philosophy. While the episcopate defended the creed of the Church against Gnosticism, and altered it in defending, it won possession of the Church herself as the reward of its chivalry.

Episcopacy had another enemy to overcome at the same time as Gnosticism, namely, Montanism. About the middle of the second century one Montanus had appeared in Phrygia as a Christian prophet, proclaiming a new revelation of the Holy Spirit. The Lord's coming is near at hand. Pepuza in Phrygia is the ' Place of Refuge,' the seat of the New Jerusalem, the place of assembly for all Christendom. All constitutional forms of the Christian Church are worthless. A Church of the ' Saints ' is to be prepared as the pure and spotless bride of the Lord. In contrast to the Church, which had already taken up her abode comfortably in this world, there burned in Montanism the fire of that hope wherewith the early Christians had looked for the speedy end of the world, united with an enthusiastic renunciation of all earthly things. Far and wide the revelation proclaimed by the new prophet was received with wild enthusiasm. Had the movement triumphed, it would have turned Christendom into a world-renouncing crowd of ascetics, and thus have stayed the mighty progress of Christian mission. It was a direct attack upon episcopacy. The bishop's authority was denied by the Montanists. The prophet alone as the immediate organ of divine revelation, not the bishop as the mere bearer of office, had authority as God's representative to receive again into the Church of the Saints those fallen into deadly sin. In Montanism the order of the early Christian Church, which knew no official privilege, was opposed to the episcopal power. But the episcopal form of constitution had already taken too deep a root in the convictions of the Church. The *Priesthood* of the bishop, which rested on his power over the spiritual life and action of the Church, more especially on his power over the celebration of the Eucharist, was victorious over Montanism. Already in the beginning of the third century the result of the contest was the complete establishment of the episcopal authority, and thereby of the principle that the bishop alone has power over his Church to administer doctrine and to exercise authority in the place of God.

The early apostolic Church was transformed into the catholic *Episcopal* Church.

With her episcopal constitution the Church put on the armour which gave her power to withstand the storms of the coming ages. What the Christian faith lost in purity of inner substance it gained in power of external organization. Ideas enter not into the world of reality unharmed.   The Church had prepared herself to gain possession of the world.   By means of her episcopal constitution she was organized after a purely temporal fashion, and set up over the growing multitude of believers a visible, ruling head.   That constitution was monarchical ; and with all the strength of monarchy the Church was able to overcome every wavering movement of the masses, as a guiding, directing, educating power.   Her enduring living force lent itself to a constitutional form for this reason : that the position of the bishop represented an object, not merely of precedent and law, but of the Church's *belief.*   In the principle : the bishop alone is the divinely appointed teacher and shepherd of the Church ; where the bishop is, there alone is the *ecclesia* ; communion with the bishop alone makes communion with Christ possible— in the spiritual meaning of this catholic principle lay the authority from which sprang the supremacy of the Church and of the Mediæval Papacy over the world. The original genuinely apostolic idea of the Church perished that her temporal supremacy might be founded ; and only after long centuries, when the catholic idea of the Church had fulfilled its mission in the world's history, could the German Reformation revive the apostolic idea of an *ecclesia*, of a universal priesthood of all believers, in order to bring forth a henceforth manly Christianity and a purified and enlightened Church, whose power is not that of external authority, but the strength of divine truth alone.

# CHAPTER III

## THE CHURCH OF THE EMPIRE

### § 11. *State and Church*

IN the year 313 Constantine, who with the comprehensive vision of a great statesman had seen the requirements of his age, gave recognition and freedom to the Church. He restored to her at the same time her worldly possessions, and protected her by numerous privileges. Paganism he left as yet untouched; it was after his time that it first met with persecution. He remained high priest (*pontifex maximus*) of the pagan worship, notwithstanding that he embraced Christianity as a catechumen receiving baptismal instruction, and was baptized in the year of his death, 337. Paganism still stood opposed to Christianity as a powerful foe; and that not merely because in the beginning of the fourth century the majority of the population throughout the Empire was still pagan. Within the pagan world there had grown up a new spiritual power—Neo-Platonism. This school, which dated from the third century, transformed the popular pagan religions into philosophy by far-fetched interpretations of their myths, and philosophy into religion through the fundamental importance which it gave to those myths. It was a renaissance of Paganism which united mysticism and speculation, and among

wide circles, especially of the educated classes, it lent
to Paganism a new splendour. The most important
result of Neo-Platonism was that by its influence the
Emperor Julian was led to turn again from Christianity
to the ancient gods. Julian the Apostate (361-363)
became once more a follower of Paganism and of the
ideals of his fathers. He undertook to set up in opposition to Christianity a Paganism revived not only in the
spirit of culture, but it may even be said in the spirit
of Christianity—a Paganism which preached a strenuous
morality and the duty of charity. Yet he did not
persecute the Christian religion. He confined himself
to granting freedom to every form of religious faith.
It was the last light that shone upon the worship of the
old gods. Yet it shone in vain. The inner power of
Paganism was extinguished. Neo-Platonism could not
replace the living power of a true religion. Under
Julian's successors Christianity was restored to its former
position as the recognized religion of the State. Paganism had no power to withstand it. It could not bring
forth martyrs. Christianity was the religion of the
future. In the course of the fifth century Paganism
has disappeared as an element of culture. *The Empire
had become Christian.* The Church had conquered.
She had been transformed from a secret society, pro-
scribed and persecuted, into the mighty and supreme
Church of the Empire, upheld by the power of the
State.

It was a triumph. But the triumph had a danger all
its own. It was not merely that, together with freedom,
honour and power, greed and ambition also found their
way into the Church. The greatest danger of all was
that the State now made good its claims upon the

Church. It had changed from a foe into an ally, but it demanded supremacy in the Church as the price of its alliance. The Roman State was not used to suffer another power to rule besides its own. It considered that not only the imperial, but the sacerdotal power, the authority of high priesthood over an official worship, belonged to it by right. The rights that it had once possessed, as against the pagan religion, it was inclined to exact from the Christian Church also. The Church was once more at war with the State. She had dared to defy the instincts of an omnipotent authority. The State might have had to yield, but now that it had protected the Church, and showered privileges and wealth upon her, it demanded all the more her absolute surrender. Thus might the friendship of the Roman State have proved more dangerous than its enmity, and in the embrace of the Empire the spiritual power of the Church ran the risk of suffocation. The right to administer ecclesiastical law, to summon general councils and to confirm their resolutions, to appoint bishops to the more important episcopal sees ; the right of supreme jurisdiction in the spiritual courts, a determining voice in all dogmatic controversies which agitated the Church, in short, the supreme government of the Church, was claimed by the Roman State, and claimed to some purpose. All the battles of the first three centuries would have been fought in vain, if now, at the last, the Church was to be degraded to a passive handmaid of the Byzantine Empire.

In spite of all, there was one advantage which the Church gained by this. Once recognized by the State, she was able to give to her own organized constitution, over the length and breadth of the Empire, a single firmly articulated form, wielding supreme power over the whole ecclesiastical order. The principle of Catholicism, which aimed at the formation of the Church according to a definite constitutional plan, had now full scope for its development. The constitution of the Church was in the main modelled on the organization of the Empire. The city (*civitas*) was the lowest political unit of the Empire. It became the lowest political unit of the Church. In the constitution of the Church the territory of the city appeared as the episcopal diocese. In the constitution of the Empire, the province, with the provincial governor, stood above the *civitas*. The episcopal dioceses were united in like manner under the direction of the metropolitan, the bishop of a provincial capital, forming an ecclesiastical province. In the constitution of the Empire, from the fourth century, several provinces composed an imperial diocese under an imperial governor (*vicarius*). The imperial diocese also (at least in certain parts of the Eastern Greek Church) formed, after the fourth century, part of the ecclesiastical constitution, as the district of a patriarch, to whom the metropolitans of the imperial dioceses were subordinate. Finally, the general union of the Churches corresponded to the general union of the Empire, with the imperial Council (the so-called Œcumenical Council) as its legitimate organ. The Church of the universal Empire was a compact unity, an outwardly visible and august embodiment of universal Christendom.

Thus in its old age the Roman Empire bequeathed its constitution to the young Church, struggling upward with all the forces of a new life. It was its last great legacy to the future. In the form of an ecclesiastical

constitution, the imperial constitution outlived the fall
of the Empire.    To this day the diocese of the Catholic
bishop is the copy of the Roman *civitas*; the province
of the Catholic archbishop the copy of the Roman
imperial province; and the Catholic Church, under a
Pope declared omnipotent by law, the copy of the
ancient Roman Empire, with its Cæsars who claimed
the world as their possession.    When the form of the
imperial constitution was stamped upon the Church,
that form, in all its venerable antiquity, its strength, its
width, and comprehension, not only perpetuated itself,
but gave to the Church its own living organic power.
With a world-embracing organization, the imperial
Church could give imposing expression to her unity;
but, what was more, had she power to save her inward
freedom and her faith?

## § 12. *The Council of Nicæa*

Ever since the end of the second century, the guidance
of the Churches had been taken by the synod which
had arisen from the meetings of individual communities,
and had grown into assemblies where the bishops of
several Churches met together.    The provincial synod,
which after the beginning of the fourth century had
become the regular organ of the Church's life, was
usually called and directed by the bishop of the
provincial capital, or metropolitan, thus laying the
foundations of the metropolitan's power over the
province.    When great and weighty questions had to
be settled, exceptionally large synods were called.
Now that the Church was recognized by the State, it
became possible to summon an imperial synod, or, as it

was called later, an Œcumenical Council, where the
bishops from all parts of the Empire met together, and
it was in a certain measure a parliament of the Church,
setting forth her unity in the most effectual manner.

A few years after Constantine had recognized the
Church, he summoned, as early as the year 325, the first
Council of the Empire, the first Council recognized as
œcumenical, that is, as representative of and regulative
for the whole Church—the Council of Nicæa.

The principal reason for calling the Council was
furnished by the great dogmatic controversy which
agitated the Church.

From the first Christianity stood face to face with
the question:—

What think ye of Christ?   Is he only David's son—
a mere man? or is he not also David's Lord—the true
God, the Lord of Hosts?

The mystery of Christ's divinity was the first and
greatest problem for the educated Christian mind.   The
whole mystery of the Church is contained in it.   The
Church is not only Christ's work, but Christ's body,
daily born anew and quickened anew by his Spirit.
In her meetings, he himself, he who is unseen and sits
at the right hand of God, is in the midst of her.   As the
nature of Christ, such is the nature and the worth of his
Church.   When the Church reflects on Christ's being
she is brought face to face with the mystery of her
own.

From the writings of Paul and John onward through
the centuries, the confession of the Christian faith is this:
that her Lord Jesus Christ is 'the First and the Last'
(Rev. i. 17); 'the beginning of the creation of God'
(Rev. iii. 14); the 'Word of God' (Rev. ix. 13), through

whom God created the whole world (1 Cor. viii. 6),
living and working in divine glory before ever the
foundations of the world were laid (1 Cor. x. 4; Phil.
ii. 6, 8); and in this sense he is both the Son of God and
God himself (John i. 14).   There were difficulties for
human thought in the fact that the Son of God who
became man, and suffered the humiliation of the flesh,
was to be conceived as distinct from God and yet equal
to God; and these difficulties had to find expression
before they could come to a solution.

Out of this difficulty there arose, in the second and
third centuries, that last great offspring of the Hellenic
spirit, Christian theology, the main facts of which were
then laid down for all ages.

Was it not possible that Jesus Christ was a mere man,
although distinguished by special gifts, by miraculous
power and holiness?   In this case there would be no
difficulty at all.   There were some who inclined to this
solution, but it never played a serious part in the history
of the Church.   At the beginning of the third century,
when it first asserted itself in Rome, it was openly
rejected by the Church and declared heretical.   Paul,
Bishop of Antioch, who held this opinion (about the
middle of the third century), was obliged to veil it from
the community by the use of orthodox formulas; notwithstanding, he was deposed and excommunicated for
his teaching by a great Eastern Council.   The divinity
of Christ was a universal assumption of theological
thought.   But God is one God.   So some (the Monarch-
ians) inferred that God the Father was incarnate in
Christ, and suffered on the cross; that God the Father,
God the Son, and God the Holy Ghost were only different and transitory revelations of the same one God:

here the distinction of the Son from the Father was given up. Others (the Subordinatianists) held the divine Being which appeared in Christ to be a spiritual being, created indeed before the world, but yet created, and therefore subordinate to the Godhead : here the essential identity of the Son and the Father was denied. But neither solution held good as orthodox, however intelligible to the understanding. The prevailing conviction which became even more decisively victorious was this :—that not only the essential identity, but the distinction of the Son and the Father was reconcilable with the unity of God.

The decisive conflict broke out in Alexandria in the beginning of the fourth century. Alexandria was both the last great nursery of Greek culture and the home of Christian theology. It was here that Origen grew *Alex* up (born 185, died during the Decian persecution, 254), the greatest theologian of the third century, who combined Greek philosophy with Christian faith. It was the place where the great questions of the age found a soil already prepared for them. It was also the place where the great and final reconciliation of Greek philosophy and Christian theology had to be accomplished once for all. Arius, a presbyter of the Alexandrian Church (some time after 313), pronounced unmistakably in favour of Subordinatianism, and drew from it the clear meaning : that the Son as created by the Father in time was like God, but yet not equal to the Father, and therefore not very God, but a being intermediate between God and man. This view, which was virtually contained in Subordinatianism, gave up in principle the divinity of Christ, even though he was declared to be not a mere man, but a higher, godlike

being revealed in human form.[1]    Arius was opposed
by Alexander, Bishop of Alexandria, who was soon
seconded by a greater than he—the deacon Athanasius,
from 328 Bishop of Alexandria.    The conflict drew
out the sympathy of the whole Church.    The Emperor
Constantine had hoped at his conversion to Christianity
to secure in the Church the firmest bond of unity for
the Empire.    His hopes would be betrayed if the
Church was now to be divided against herself.    In
order to put an end to the strife, after all other means
of reconciliation had failed, he determined to summon
the Council of Nicæa (325).    Here, in a meeting of
bishops from all parts of the Empire, the decision which
should guide the Church was to be made.    It was made
in favour of the faith which Athanasius defended, but
not without help from the influence of the Emperor.
But that it was not imperial caprice which gave the
casting vote may readily be seen.    Constantine himself
changed his opinion.    His successor in the East professed Arianism.    Constantius was decidedly inclined
to Arianism, and in his reign of eight years (353-361)
over the West as well, he combated the Nicene faith
with all the means in his power.    Arianism was
victorious in the East.    But in the West the Nicene
confession was powerful, even in the midst of persecution
and apostasy.    Here the main current of the Church's
creed held its course undiverted by the influence of
Greek speculation.    Even in the East, Arianism could
not permanently maintain its power.    After gaining

[1] The Arian view was therefore known as the doctrine of the *likeness*
of essence (ὁμοιούσιον), the Athanasian view (accepted at the Council of
Nicæa) as the doctrine of the *identity* of essence (ὁμοούσιον) of the Father
and the Son.

the upper hand through the support of the Emperor,
it split into various parties. The second Œcumenical
Synod of Constantinople (381), by the help of the
Athanasian Emperor Theodosius, once more declared
the Nicene confession to be the confession of the whole
Church. Arianism became extinct of itself. It had
not that strength of resistance which the storms of
history demand. It was the first attempt (naturally a
failure) to replace the faith of Christianity by a dialectic
rationalism. The Nicene doctrine of the distinction
and yet identity of essence of the Father and the Son,
which was then formally expressed in the doctrine of
the Trinity, of the divine unity in three Persons,
conquered, because it leaves the incomprehensible still
incomprehensible, and reveals, while it reverently
hides, the wonderful mystery of Christ's person. The
divinity of Christ was of old the creed and the hope of
the Church. It had now merely become clearer what
a marvellous riddle had been given to mankind to read.
The mystery was shown, and confessed to be a mystery;
and in mystery religion has alike its essence and its
power.

Yet another phase in the development of thought
found completion through Athanasius and the Nicene
confession. Thirst for the knowledge of that which

> 'holds the world in every part
> Together at its inmost heart,'

was the very soul of ancient philosophy. Redemption
seemed to be implied in that knowledge: comprehend
the world, so shall you be freed from it. Thus the
philosopher of the ancient world was his own saviour.
He had no need of any other. Christian theology at

its rise was also ruled by this fundamental idea of ancient philosophy. Origen's great master, Clement of Alexandria, was author of the bold saying, that the wise man, if knowledge could be offered to him in one hand and salvation in the other, would refuse eternal salvation if only he might gain the knowledge of God. Origen took a determined stand upon the Old and New Testaments, that he might be the first to found on the Canon (now firmly established) a system of living, scriptural theology that should endure for all time; but notwithstanding his determination, even he remained convinced that the historical Jesus Christ, with his birth and sufferings and death, with all the great work of salvation done by him, was a necessity only for the sinful multitude. The wise man, the philosopher, according to Origen also, had no need of a Saviour, but only of the Divine Teacher and Revealer of Truth. This Hellenizing theology, which strove before all things after knowledge, after the satisfaction of the intellect, found its appropriate expression in Subordinatianism. To this Hellenizing theology, even to that of Origen, Christ is the incarnation of the rational law (the 'Logos' of the philosophers) that works in the world, its governor and creator. Christ is the incarnate Law of Nature, the law of all material, as of all spiritual and moral things. He is the totality of all thought, of all laws realized in the universe, the 'Idea of ideas.' This Christ is conceived, in the first place, as the divine power active in creation. The whole creation is from the beginning contained in Christ, in the thought of the world, the Logos proceeding from God; and the interest of the 'wise man,' even of philosophical theologians like Clement of

Alexandria and Origen, is concentrated above all on this eternal Logos, who creates and governs, lightens and *en*lightens the world. In the contemplation of the divine reason living in the world, the wise man, even the Alexandrian theologian of the third century, found, like the ancient Stoic and Platonist, that peace of mind which freed him from the world, and was in this sense his salvation. Even the theology of Clement and Origen ends like ancient philosophy in Gnostic *salvation through self*. It is obvious that such a theology is only another form of Subordinatianism. As the ideal source of creation, as the cosmic principle—a principle which is no longer a unity, but contains in itself the multiplicity of the universe—Christ is of necessity a divine person subordinate to the Father.

Christian theology in the third century, through the influence of the great Alexandrian theologians, Clement and Origen, was in danger of being turned into a new 'Gnosis,' into Hellenic philosophy. It was the great work of Athanasius to combat this rapidly advancing development of thought with all the force alike of his faith and his philosophic learning. Athanasius was the first to raise into the sphere of philosophic science the two principles of Christianity—the fact that Christianity came into the world to bring, not salvation of self through the knowledge of self and of the world, but salvation through Christ. The idea of salvation through Christ, through a deed wrought by God and not by us, is the central point of the whole system of Athanasian theology. It rests, like the theology of Paul, upon the thought that life and blessedness come not by knowledge of the world, but by the *forgiveness of sins*. The Hellenic thought of the Logos-Christ,

the Creator of the world, disappears before the Logos
of St. John's Gospel, the Son of the living God, the
*Saviour* of the world. The salvation of a sinful world
can be accomplished through no other being than God
himself, and the Saviour Christ must be equal to God.
If God himself were not the source of our salvation
we were yet in our sins. This longing for a salvation
wrought by God, a longing which is not philosophical,
but religious and wholly Christian, is the strength of the
Nicene or Athanasian doctrine. Through this strength
it has won the world over to its side. The great
contest which was brought to a peaceable close by
means of the Nicene Council was not a barren dispute
about words, not a struggle to introduce one more
speculative idea (that of the ὁμοούσιον) into theology.
It was a struggle for the final expulsion of pagan
philosophy from Christian territory, that the essence
of Christianity might not be sought in a logical ex-
planation of the universe, nor its result in the establishment of a philosophical theory. Speculation was to be
divested of that power which all ancient philosophy,
even the Alexandrian theology of the third century, had
given to it—the power to bring man into relation with
the divine by means of his own reflective thought. The
Hellenization of Christianity was successfully combated
by Athanasius and the Nicene Council. A great
danger lay in the fact that Christian theology at the
first had begun, and was obliged to begin, by following
the intellectual methods of traditional pagan philosophy. This danger was now happily overcome. While
salvation through Christ was made the central point
of theological thought without turning Christianity into
philosophy, the subject-matter of Christianity—that

true and eternal content, which brings comfort and deliverance, and which belongs to Christianity as a religion—was comprehended as matter of science, and at the same time was set in full light as the revelation of the acts of grace wrought by God for sinful humanity. In this sense the Nicene confession was the regeneration of the Gospel, and thereby the firm foundation of the whole future development of the Church.

## § 13. *Institution of Patriarchs*

The Council of Nicæa was also concerned with the organization of the Church. The authority of the bishop of the provincial capital (the metropolitan), together with the provincial synods, over the bishops and Churches of the province, was the principle of ecclesiastical constitution which was adopted at Nicæa. But there were single large bishoprics, whose already existing authority overstepped the narrow limits of the imperial province. The Council confirmed the traditional privileges of these individual Churches. Those mentioned by name were the three Churches of Rome, Alexandria, and Antioch. They were the Churches of the three great capitals of the Roman Empire. Alexandria had legal authority over Egypt and the adjoining countries, Antioch authority over Syria and the neighbouring portions of the Eastern Empire, Rome over Italy.

The Bishop of Constantinople now appeared as a new power in the constitution of the Church. When Constantinople became the second capital of the Empire, it was natural that its bishop should claim a place beside the bishops of other great cities, the more so because his direct relations with the imperial authority made the high position of the Bishop of Byzantium as much the interest of the Empire as the advancement of the bishop of the imperial capital. At the Council of Constantinople, in the year 381, a rank in the Church, second only to that of the Bishop of Rome, was given unconditionally to the Bishop of Constantinople. At the Council of Chalcedon (451) the three imperial dioceses of Thrace, Asia (that is, Asia Minor), and Pontus, were made subject to him as his dominion, so that the bishops of Heraclea, Ephesus, and Cæsarea ranked henceforth merely as exarchs, in subordination to the Patriarch of Constantinople.

The Bishop of Jerusalem also was noticed with honour by the Council of Nicæa. In order to confer distinction on the Mother-Church of Christendom, he was raised by the Council of Chalcedon to the rank of Patriarch of Palestine.

It was the title of Patriarch which, after the second half of the fifth century, distinguished the five great Sees of Rome, Constantinople, Alexandria, Antioch, and Jerusalem. The guidance of the Christian Church lay in their hands. But the meaning of their new title was this: that each one of them had right to the rank of 'Great Father,' or Pope, of all Christendom. And now there appeared on the horizon the question of a monarchical Head of the Church, of the œcumenical *ecclesia* furnished by law with supreme authority. The great question suggested by the title of Patriarch was this: Who among all these great bishops shall be the first, the *Primate of the whole Church*?

## § 14. *Rome and Constantinople*

The Bishop of Constantinople came forward rapidly into power. From the position of a simple bishop, subject to the Bishop of Heraclea, he was raised in the course of the fourth century to the rank of one of the first bishops in Christendom. The Council of Chalcedon (451), which had placed three imperial dioceses under him, had at the same time given him supreme jurisdiction and authority over the remaining Churches, and thus over the whole of Christendom. The great question was already decided: not one of the great, the ancient and renowned apostolic sees, but this, their latest offspring, barely born, the See of Constantinople, was to be the first in all Christendom, the Bishop of Constantinople was to be the Bishop of all bishops, the Primate of the Church.

The change was sudden. How did it become possible?

Not in vain did the Bishop of Constantinople become bishop of the second imperial capital, which, with the disruption of the Western Roman Empire, took more and more the position of the first. Towards the end of the fifth century the Western Empire fell, after it had long become but the shadow of an Empire. The East-Roman Emperor in Constantinople was now the Emperor of the whole world. Why should he not claim the rights of a ruler of the world? According to the natural instincts of the Roman Empire, power over the Church was among the rights of a ruler of the world. The Bishop of Constantinople was bishop at the Court of the Emperor, moving in the sphere of majesty itself, the creature of the imperial will, and as an ecclesiastic the more incapable of independent action because his see depended on no ancient ecclesiastical traditions or privileges. What the Bishop of Constantinople was, and what he represented in the Church, he owed to the Emperor. All the more, therefore, was it worth while to advance him. What was gain to the Bishop of Constantinople was gain to the Emperor. Soaring on eagle's wings, the imperial power bore the Bishop of Constantinople with it upwards. In the person of the Bishop of Constantinople, the Empire more than ever gained authority over the Church. The decisions of Constantinople (381) and of Chalcedon (451) meant that henceforth neither the Bishop of Rome, nor the Bishop of Alexandria, nor any other bishop, but the *Emperor, was the supreme head of the Church.* The whole development of the Church's constitution seemed to have been in vain : the fabric of her organization was made, as it were, a crown for an earthly head.

Was there any power in the Church, ready and able to withstand the Empire, and to defend the self-government of the Church through a supreme spiritual head against the ruler of the world ?

That was the great place in the world's history which was filled by the Bishop of Rome. He it was who undertook the battle with Constantinople, and who alone could undertake it. All natural resources of ecclesiastical power which Rome already possessed would of necessity increase his influence twofold, seeing that the cause of Rome was the cause of the Church's freedom.

From the second half of the second century the Roman Church was supposed to have been founded by the apostles Paul and Peter. The Roman Bishop was held to be the successor of Peter, the prince of apostles.

If Peter was the rock on which the Church was built, then henceforth (now that the idea of the succession from Peter had arisen) the Bishop of Rome must be the rock of the Church. Where was another bishop who could be compared with him?

It soon became customary to hold counsel with the great Churches in all weighty matters affecting the ecclesiastical commonwealth. The decision which proceeded from an apostolic Church (a Church founded by the apostles) was of special authority. It was there that the true doctrine of the apostles would be preserved in its purest form. Rome was the single apostolic Church in all the West. It stood in unbroken relations with Africa (that is, with Latin Africa, with Carthage for its centre), Spain, and Gaul; it delivered decisions, the authority of which was felt even when they were contested, and it assumed unconditional rank above all Churches.

Before all, Rome was the capital of the world, the eternal city, *the* city above all others. From the time of the apostle Paul, who would have considered the great work of his mission to the Gentiles unfinished if he had not laboured in Rome and established relations with the Roman community (and at this time neither the apostle Peter, nor any representative, to say nothing of a successor, of Peter was to be found in Rome!). Through all the centuries onwards may be seen the supreme position taken in the Church, not first of all by the Roman Bishop, but by the Roman community. The Roman community was beyond dispute the first, the most important, and the most influential of all the Churches in Christendom, even for the East. All doctrinal controversies of the first three centuries were finally decided by the Roman Church. Monarchical Episcopacy (*supra*, page 37), together with ecclesiastical law and Catholicism, had their origin in Rome. From the end of the first century, Catholicism with its legalised constitutional and doctrinal forms, has spread from Rome outwards, over the whole circle of the Christian globe. The Roman Church is the Mother-Church of Catholic Christendom. The enormous means which she had at her disposal, by reason of the large number of her members, and the great wealth of many of them, gave to her spiritual rank an economic background. Not only in the West, but in Greece and Asia, there went forth the fame both of her orthodoxy and of her readiness to help. It was impossible but that after the rise of the Episcopate the power of the Church should be transferred to her bishop. Already, towards the end of the second century, the Bishop of Rome could undertake to proceed against the Church of Asia Minor with excommunication, on account of some irregularity in the celebration of the Easter festival.

By right of ecclesiastical primogeniture the Bishop of Rome prepared to contest the claims of Constantinople, which represented the claims of the Empire. The promotion of Constantinople to the rank of second capital of the Empire was the first great stroke aimed at the rising power of the Bishop of Rome. Rome had ceased to be the capital of the Empire, the centre of the world. The more the Roman Empire found its centre of gravitation in the East, the more would the Bishop of Constantinople become the supreme spiritual head round whom the Grecian nations of the East could rally. This was expressed unmistakably in the decisions of Constantinople (381) and Chalcedon (451).

The protests of the Roman legates resounded unceasingly through the East.  That Rome did not owe her
position mainly to the apostles Paul and Peter, but to
her character as the capital of the world, was made clear
in that moment when a second capital of the Empire
sprang up beside her.

Notwithstanding, it was in this time of conflict with
Constantinople, that the foundations were laid of that
high position on which rests all the later history of the
Bishop of Rome.

Even in the fourth century Rome was able to derive
no small advantage therefrom.  The Arian controversy
had been peaceably settled at the Council of Nicæa.
But in vain.  Under the leadership of Constantine's
Arian successor, the whole of the East arose in defence
of Arianism (p. 52).  Athanasius was deposed from
his Alexandrian bishopric by the Synod of Tyre (335),
and a second time by a Synod at Antioch (340).  The
West alone, under the leadership of Rome, remained
true to the Nicene faith.  So Athanasius fled to Rome
to plead his cause there ; and the Roman bishop, Julius,
declared at a Roman Synod that Athanasius had been
unjustly deposed, and forthwith restored him to his
bishopric.  The Roman bishop and his synod exercised
authority over all Christendom.  Athanasius was not
the only one who appealed to Rome.  The fresh conflicts which continually arose between the Arian
countries of the East and the few Oriental bishops who
remained true to the orthodox faith, gave repeated
opportunities to Rome to interfere as umpire in the
disputes even of the Greek Church.  It was of no great
consequence that the judgment of Rome (as in the
restoration of Athanasius) was by no means recognized

as final by the opposing bishops of the East. The fact remained that the Western bishops under oppression appealed to Rome as the umpire of the Church ; and that the Roman Church with her claims became henceforward conspicuous in the sight of the whole Church. She even succeeded in gaining a decision of Council in her favour. In the year 343, an imperial, that is, an œcumenical, Synod was again summoned at Sardica (Sofia in Bulgaria). The bishops were divided on the question of faith, so that the Council split up, and the Arian bishops of the East adjourned to Philippopolis, to hold a separate Synod there. But the Council of Sardica, now become a Latin and Western synod, recognised the right of the Bishop of Rome to hear appeals on behalf of deposed bishops, and to sanction the meeting of a new synod, that is, another provincial synod, to deliver a new verdict as to the justice of the deposition. At the Synod of Sardica the West was the fortress in which dwelt the power of the Papacy ; and the West solemnly recognised the right of its leading bishop to exercise authority over the whole Church.

At the close of the fourth century, the great doctrinal contest ended in the defeat of Arianism. The victory of the Nicene faith was the victory of Rome. Were not all the great bishoprics of the East tainted with damnable heresy? What other Church but Rome had unfurled in all battles the banner of orthodoxy?

And now, at a time when Rome must have felt herself more than ever justified in taking the government of the whole Church into her own hands, was an upstart like the Bishop of Constantinople—what was more, was the temporal power—to be suffered thus unjustly to snatch the great prize for itself? For

Rome the Empire had already begun to lose its terrors. The great flood of the German nations was pouring in far and wide over the already defenceless West. For the Western Church the fall of the Empire was deliverance from an overbearing temporal authority. The West, as the immediate territory of the Bishop of Rome, was beyond the power of the will that ruled in Constantinople. Yet there came a time, in the sixth and seventh centuries, when the Bishop of Rome was brought low, and held in unworthy subjection to the Emperor and to the Bishop of the East, the Bishop of Constantinople. But the Frankish kingdom was to come, to deliver the Bishop of Rome, and to restore to him, once for all, his primacy over the Latin half of the Empire.

By the Council of Chalcedon (451) the primacy of Constantinople was decreed. The legates of the Roman bishop who were present delivered a solemn protest. The challenge was given to the combat, and the two combatants stood face to face. The course of the world's history depended on the issue of their conflict. It laid the foundations of that great opposition which, in later times, divided the Church into two communions: the Roman Catholic, and the Greek Catholic Church.

With such discord closes the history of the first centuries. Yet all Christendom forms a great ecclesiastical unity, an enormous, world-embracing horizon. Strong and high rises the tree sprung from the grain of mustard seed, yielding its life-giving fruit far and wide, so that the nations come and lodge in the branches thereof. But already on the horizon the storm-clouds are lowering from which the thunder-bolt shall come

forth, to cleave the proud trunk in twain. Only because
of the ambition of two bishops? Only because the
Roman Empire was once divided into a Latin half and
a Greek half, and a second capital sprung up beside the
ancient imperial capital? Not so. The cleavage of the
Church was the first great step in her onward development. That cleavage had to be, in order to make
possible the whole glorious history of the Church of the
middle ages, and to deliver the West from the East—
from a world already sinking into the sleep of death.

## § 15. *Rise of Monasticism—Augustine*

The final separation of the Western and Eastern
Churches was proclaimed. At the same time there
appeared those spiritual forces which were to give to
the Western Church her independent character and
power of development.

In the course of the fourth century Monasticism arose.
It was the sign of a great popular movement which bore
blazoned on its banner one word—'Renunciation.'
There had been ascetics before, who had held themselves
bound to renounce marriage, property, and the enjoyment of flesh and wine, for Christ's sake; and the gift
of asceticism passed for a *charisma* or gift of the Holy
Spirit; but only for one *charisma* among others, not for
a special *charisma* with a value belonging to it alone.
It was a new departure when the highest worth came
to be ascribed to asceticism as such. The theory
which was the supreme principle of Pagan philosophy,
that sense, as sense, is immoral, and that the subjection
of the bodily passions through 'Ecstasy,' that is, through
detachment from the body, can alone lead the spirit of

the wise man to God—this theory took captive the
Christian world also. Asceticism was now declared to
be a duty of life ; nay, more, to be the highest duty of
life, inasmuch as it was a means to the vision and
possession of God. Monasticism arose in the moment
when this thought was shared by the masses of the
people, and multitudes withdrew into the solitude of
the deserts that they might make asceticism the calling
of their life. These masses became gradually organized ;
and in the cloister which arose in the wilderness without, an organized Asceticism sprung up beside the
organized Church. The two powers which were to
rule the future appeared in the arena ; each founded on
opposite principles, yet each related to the other. The
Church was transformed into an institution in which
salvation depended on a certain fixed organization, and
which, through its priesthood and its sacramental
powers, sustained, purified, and sanctified the life of the
individual. In Monasticism there appeared, as against
the constitutional Church, the free power of the *individual*, who set out on his own path that he might work
out *his own* salvation. The Church recognised Monasticism, and was obliged to recognise it, although at
heart it implied a contradiction of the principle—
fought for so bitterly and so long—of salvation by
means of the constitutional Catholic Church alone
(*extra ecclesiam nulla salus*) ; although the monk fled
from the secularized Church of the fourth century, as
he had fled from the secular world.

For the Church herself, Monasticism was in a certain
measure a safety-valve through which the superfluous
spiritual forces (the claims of which had not been
adequately provided for in the Church's programme for

life) might escape and find room for their development without breaking through existing ecclesiastical forms. Before all, Monasticism was the only form in which the individual could find, not alone his peace with God, but an aim to be striven for, a way to higher ideals, and a means towards a far-reaching practical activity. The principles of the Church's organisation, like those of her doctrine, were unchangeable. In his Monastery, in his Order alone, could the individual, as such, find a field for the unfolding of his talents, a field for his life which admitted of his full development through all the forces of his personality. In the Church it was her power of persistence that mainly told. In Monasticism, the impulse towards progress outweighed all other. Monasticism, which was irresistibly attractive to those who were spiritually strongest, was, in spite of its voluntary flight from the world and the Church, expressly fitted from the first to be the Church's leader.

Towards the middle of the fourth century Monasticism appeared already in an organised form in Lower Egypt. From thence it passed directly into the East. Towards the end of the fourth century it made its entry into the West under the leadership of Jerome. To the educated classes, with their love of art and science, their inborn sense of all that was graceful in the cultivation of life, the monastic orders of the third and fourth centuries, with their self-torture and self-neglect, their uncleanliness and utter absence of all culture, appeared in the sharpest contrast, and were first met by contempt and determined repulsion. It was seen that the aim of Christianity was not the degradation and enslaving of the personality, but its completion and fulfilment. But there yet failed that clear, religious

conviction of the worthlessness of Monasticism as a
contradiction of the Gospel, a conviction which Martin
Luther first won for the world a thousand years later.
Those who then opposed themselves to Monasticism
were actuated far more by worldly than by spiritual
interests. Therefore they were defeated. All the
strength of a religious life was in those days on the side
of the ascetics. They sought their salvation with fear
and trembling. They were possessed by a living force
of conviction that was actually ready to count all this
world's gain as nothing for Christ's sake. For this
cause the Church was bound to be on their side. In
the sixth century the battle was already decided, and
decided in favour of Monasticism. The Church had
submitted to the monastic ideal. The path of the
Church's history entered, as it were, the sign of Monasticism. The catholicization of Christendom was thereby
completed.

In the East, Monasticism has assuredly to this day
remained true to its ideal of pure renunciation, of a life
devoted to contemplation and asceticism, estranged
from the world and the world's culture. But only in
rare instances has it influenced the Church's history,
and that mainly by its force of inertia, by the strength
of fanatical resistance with which it opposed every
innovation, whether in dogma or in worship. The
iconoclastic enterprises of the Greek emperors in the
eighth and ninth centuries, for instance, were wrecked
on this rock.

But in Western Monasticism the powers of the individual unfolded their full life and strength. Latin
Monasticism became the supreme power which guided
the further development of the Church, which bore

upward the Latin Church, laid the foundations of the Papacy, and afterwards brought about the great work of the Reformation.

Western Monasticism received its characteristic form through Benedict of Nursia, the founder and first abbot of the Monastery of Monte Cassino (built between Subiaco and Naples in 528). The rule of the Benedictines became the typical rule for the monasteries of the West. The rules of all later Orders are founded on it. The characteristic of the Benedictine rule was the place it gave to labour in the monastic programme. True, labour had been recognized from the first as a means towards asceticism. The monk was to labour, not for the sake of the result, but for his own sake, for the sake of his moral self-discipline and moral health. But the labour of the Benedictine monk was destined to change the solitudes which surrounded the cloisters into seats of learning and culture. It was to prepare a place in the cloister for art and training. It was to turn the cloisters into centres of education, from which there should go forth into the world influences all-powerful in the practical, intellectual, and spiritual life. As a society of workers the Benedictines were to turn their faces towards the world. These ascetics were irresistibly compelled by community of labour to proceed from the renunciation of the world to the education of the world, to the reformation of the household, the State, and the Church.

Besides Monasticism, which in the fifth century was preparing for the conquest of the West, there appeared about the same time an individual spirit, likewise destined to be the ruling intellectual force in the development of the Western Church—Augustine (died

as Bishop of Hippo in Africa, 430). To him it was given
to sound all the depths and heights of spiritual experience in his own soul, to prove in his inmost heart the
consoling power of the Gospel, out of sin and agony of
conscience to reach the blessedness of communion with
God, like Paul and Luther. While it was yet early he
arose, like a giant in his strength, to shake off the bonds
wherewith earthly pleasure and sensuality had bound
him, and win the grace of God and deliverance from
the burden of sin. One after another he had explored
all the systems of religion which filled the world in his
time. He became a student, first of Manichæism (the
latest form of Semitic Paganism), then of Neo-
Platonism. Manichæism, by offering to the finished
ascetic, as the latest secret, its crudely naturalistic
doctrine of the God of Light, and of Light as the power
of the good, left him in a state of disenchantment, even
of despair. Neo-Platonism led him to Christianity, by
giving him, in his despair of finding truth, a new hope
of salvation and communion with God. Here he found
what he had so long sought with passionate fervour—
the living God who forgiveth sins. The divine truth
which is made manifest in Jesus Christ, the power of
divine love poured out in pity on the sinner, made
their triumphal entry into his heart. On Easter Eve
387, at the age of thirty-three, he was baptized by the
great Bishop Ambrose at Milan. The duty of his life
was henceforth twofold : to proclaim, first, the gospel
of sin and grace, and then the glory of the Church.
Against the British monk Pelagius he developed the
doctrine of Original Sin and of the salvation of man by
Grace alone ; making the doctrine of Grace, as Luther
at first also made it, equivalent to the doctrine of

Predestination.   Against the African Donatists, who
would have made the effectual working of the Sacraments dependent on the worthiness of the minister, he
set up the idea of the Church as an institution for
dispensing salvation, an institution possessing *objective*
sanctity.   The supreme value of the Church—even of
the outwardly visible Church constituted as she is—he
expressed in the statement that she represents the
'City of God' (*Civitas Dei*) upon earth.   From this
commonwealth salvation flows forth upon the individual.   To serve this commonwealth, and in particular
to lead back the erring (the Donatists) by force into
the Church, is the highest duty of the State.   Only by
doing such service to the Church will the State attain
a value which does not otherwise belong to it.   The
middle ages are dawning.   Catholicism, at least
Western Catholicism, in claiming supremacy for the
Church over the world, is embodied for the first time
in Augustine's mighty personality.   Even in his
monkish convictions he is a Catholic.   Flight from
the world into the cloister is to him the perfection of
the Christian life.

Yet this man has the Reformation—Luther's Reformation—in him too.   Side by side with his conception
of the Church as a hierarchy, he holds the opposite
idea of the true Church as the invisible Church of the
predestined—the redeemed.   In direct contradiction to
his doctrine of the saving power of the Church, he
lives by faith in grace freely given by God as the
only source of salvation.   He prepared a way for
Catholicism by his doctrine of the Church, for Luther
by his doctrine of Sin and Grace.   The extremes
which Augustine was able to unite stand historically

opposed to each other in two great ecclesiastical bodies.

The theology of Augustine did a priceless service to the Western world, in freeing it from the intellectual despotism of the East. Out of the depths of a Christian individuality which had truly and in itself experienced salvation through Christ, was poured forth, with abounding fulness of thought, and commanding force of intellect and language, a stream of religious ideas and problems which have made the life of the Western Church fruitful for all future time. Augustine influenced all later times, on the one hand through the force of a mighty *subjectivity*, which by striving for the possession of God with an increasing longing, attained at last to a personal experience of the love of God in Christ, and to rest in a firm assurance of divine grace; on the other hand, through the dogmatic determination with which he nevertheless established the authority of the Church as an *objective* fact, in order to make it the final basis of any certainty of salvation.

The West is nearing the age of its spiritual majority. Western Monasticism and Augustinian theology are the two powers which shall henceforth guide it. One thing alone is yet wanting to bring in a new age—the fertilisation of the Latin world by means of the German nations that were now entering on the stage of history in all the freshness of their youth.

# Division II

# THE MIDDLE AGES

## § 16. INTRODUCTION

WHEN we leave the Church history of the earlier centuries for that of the Middle Ages we enter on a new stage of lesser relative proportions. The horizon of mediæval Church history is no longer that of Christendom ; it is only the horizon of the West. It is to the West that the history of the world has shifted its centre of gravity—to Italy, Spain, Gaul, Britain, Germany, where with mighty throes the Western Teutonic-Roman people is to be born, the people that is to rule the future.

The Middle Ages begin with a tremendous process of destruction. In the East the advance of Islam gave a death-blow to the Greek Church, and with the Church to the national character and culture of Greece. Like a stream of fire devouring all life before it, the troops of the Mohammedan conquerors poured forth over Asia and Africa. In the seventh century the movement began (the first appearance of Mohammed was in the year 611) ; in the beginning of the eighth century it had already reached Spain (the kingdom of Spain was overthrown by the Moors, 711). A few years later

(732), when it was opposed by Karl Martell with the united strength of the Frankish kingdom, the same power was waiting on the banks of the Loire, ready to overflood the whole West, and to deal with Roman-Teutonic Church and culture as it had dealt with the Church and culture of the East.

The Greek nation had lost its powers of life. It was a nation more richly endowed than any that has been before or after it; where the very porter in the streets philosophized; where the barbers' shops and the taverns echoed to the sound of disputes about the mysteries of faith; where not only religion, but theology, was made popular, and stirred the multitude itself to wild excitement; where intellectual life, to which the conquering force of the whole nation contributed, seemed inexhaustible in its energy—this nation, the richest, the most glorious and wonderful of all nations, was overthrown, trodden down and trampled under foot, never more to rise up again. In the East, in the place of Hellenic culture, there appeared Arabian culture, itself an intellectual power far beyond the middle ages in mathematical and physical science, and in philosophy, and which had a powerful influence on the Western world in bringing forth mediæval Scholasticism; a culture which, for all its sober subtlety of intellect, and the radiant glamour of Oriental poetry which surrounded it as with an imperishable glory, was yet a culture of the second order only, not worthy to be compared with that of ancient Hellas, destitute as it was of purity of form, of the Promethean force of genius, and, above all, of that sense of history which gives to investigation its spur, its freedom, its power of vision and an unbounded field of view. The work of the Renaissance, at the end of the Middle Ages, was to deliver us from a mediæval culture so strongly influenced by Arabia, and to awaken the science and the culture of our own time.

The Greek nation was no more: it never recovered from that fearful blow.

With the Greek nation there fell the Greek Church.

True, there yet stood the Patriarchal Sees of Alexandria, Antioch, and Jerusalem, where Islam granted toleration to the remnant of the Church. But its power of development was destroyed, both in Byzantium and in Alexandria. The single event which once more shook the power of the Greek Church was the attempt of the Greek emperors at iconoclastic reform, in the eighth and ninth centuries. Image-worship, which came so near to idolatry, was to be prevented by the complete banishment of images from the churches. The Emperor hoped to win over the Jews and Mohammedans of the Empire to the communion of a Church thus purified. One faith, one Church, was to be the firm bond of union for the Empire. With this thought Leo the Isaurian began the movement (717-741). But the power of Monasticism and the superstitious needs of the people were stronger than the Emperor and his army. The great Bishops of Jerusalem, Antioch, and Alexandria, with the Bishop of Rome at their head, who were now beyond the power of the Emperors, declared themselves in favour of the worship of images; and this was decisive. A great Synod at Nicæa (the seventh œcumenical council), in the year 787, decided the victory for the '*worship*' (*dulia*) of images, which was to be referred to the object of the images, and distinguished from the '*adoration*' of God (*latria*). Roman as well as Greek Catholicism has ever since remained firmly by this standpoint. About the middle of the ninth century the Empire began its retreat. The last of the Iconoclasts was Theophilus, Emperor of Constantinople (829-842). The victory was won, and the Greek Church sank into apathy, as Monasticism had sunk. John of Damascus (died some time after 754, a monk in the cloister of Saba near Jerusalem), one of the leaders of the image-worshipping party, embodied the dogmas of the Greek Church in a systematic philosophical and theological work, which, besides summing up the work of the Greek Church, helped to lay the foundations of mediæval scholasticism. It was the last significant intellectual product of Greek Christendom. From that time all is silence, and with the extinction of its intellectual life the Church fell finally into dependence on the State. The papal power of the Byzantine Empire conquered in spite of the victory which the ecclesiastical powers had won in the iconoclastic controversy. The Church had maintained its essence, its dogma, and its worship, but its powers of government were sunk in the imperial government of the State. The candlesticks of the Greek Church were removed. All that was yet left of her under the sceptre of the Eastern Roman Emperor had just life enough to hand over the alphabet and elements of culture, together with the doctrine of the Church, as a last legacy to the Sclavonic races which were streaming in on all sides. But the Sclavonic people had no power to bring the Greek world to a new birth. The Greek Church and the Greek world remained dead. The Greek Church of to-day, as we see it before us in Russia, and in the bordering countries of the Balkan Peninsula, is the Church of the seventh century turned to stone. Not a step further has been taken.  Just as history left it at the time of the great war of extermination in the seventh century, do we find it to this day, more than a thousand years later.  The Greek Church lies rigid and cold in death.  When will the Spirit from above awaken her, that was once so glorious, to a new life?

In the beginning of the Middle Ages the Western world also offers a picture of dissolution.  The Empire has fallen, the mighty Empire which once ruled the world.  The hosts of the German nations have stormed in over the West, destroying and laying waste, carrying their barbarism outward from the primeval forests of Germany into the rich countries of the civilised world. Night has come down.  All that was once glorious, great, and beautiful, all that completed life and made it worth living—art, learning, the wide-ruling power of the Empire—all is ruined.  That ruin, was it not the ruin of the world itself?

Night had come, and nowhere was there any sign of a new dawn.

Yet one ground of hope was left.  The Empire indeed was fallen, but not the Church.  In the East the Church had been laid waste together with the Empire ; and, with the Church, whatever culture yet remained rooted in it had lost its strength.  But in the West the Church stood steadfast.  In a world of ruins, in the midst of the general destruction, it stood as the sole witness to the past.  It rescued its organization, its traditions, and its faith from the ancient world and delivered them to the new age.  Through its preaching, as through its constitution, it conquered the conqueror himself.  The Germans made their entry into the vast halls of the Christian Church, in order—as Remigius, Bishop of

Rheims, said to the Frankish king Clovis—'to worship ∿
that which they had once persecuted, to persecute that
which they had once worshipped.' The Church was
saved, and culture was saved with her. The whole
culture of the ancient world, the whole of that wealth
which it had laid up for the world of the future, was
to remain unlost. In the silent cells of the cloister,
beneath the sheltering wing of the Church, with her
band of monkish students and scholars, the precious
treasure was guarded, till the time first came when it
could be brought forth once more, to enrich a new world.
The German races received Christianity with all the
strength and intensity of German feeling. German
blood was noble enough, and had enough of living
power, to fashion anew the world and the Church of the
West. Upon the Teutonic-Roman nation, which now
arose in the West from the fusion of the Latin and
German races, the progress of the world's history
depends. In earlier times it was the Greek Church that
was the leader of Christendom ; but now the sceptre has
been yielded into the hands of the Latins.

Mediæval Church history, which embraces Western
Christendom only, has a narrowly bounded horizon,
yet a horizon which comprehends the whole development of the future.

# CHAPTER I

## THE FRANKISH EMPIRE

### § 17. *The Kingdoms of the Germans*

THE Kingdoms of the Germans have arisen in succession on the ruins of the Roman Empire. To which of them shall the palm be given? Which of them shall succeed in raising up again what was destroyed, in creating anew, on Roman soil, and in the form of a German State, the glorious and unforgotten Empire in its might and world-wide sovereignty? The Empire had fallen; but the idea of an empire still stood like a sun in the firmament, and shone above the horizon through all the Middle Ages. For many a long century, to the invading barbarians the Roman Empire remained the ideal of all that was great and glorious. It held them captive as with a magic spell; and long after the Roman Empire had vanished, it was followed by the yearning of the conquerors who had destroyed it. To them the Empire was the one and only State—the ideal, the incomparable, nay, more, the indispensable, the imperishable, and eternal State. The history of the Empire seemed but another name for the history of mankind. To rear again this Empire, to restore to humanity the perfect form of its political life, was to be the great, the highest aim of German statesmanship.

Not merely in the brains of scholars, but in the imagination of the people, there lived that dream of empire which was the direct result of all that in the times of the Roman Empire had been seen, experienced, and received, never to be lost again ; a dream in which were woven mysterious, dazzling pictures ; which with its intoxicating power impelled men onwards to immortal deeds, and had strength to bring forth, first the Frankish, then the German Empire.

By which of the German kingdoms was the Empire to be upraised again ? By the kingdom of the East-Goths, or of the West-Goths ? of the Vandals, or of the Burgundians ? The answer of history was : By none of these, but by the Kingdom of the Franks.

One fact was decisive for this end from the very first. The united German races, which up to this time had any dealings with the Roman Empire, had embraced Christianity in the form of Arianism. The Eastern Empire was Arian in the greater part of the fourth century, while at the same time, on the banks of the Danube, first the Goths, then the remaining races akin to the Goths—the Vandals, Burgundians, Alans, and Sueves—learned Christianity from the Eastern Empire. Thus after Arianism had been already extinguished in the Roman Empire, it lived a further iife among the converted German races. Not that the masses of the Gothic or Vandal peasants had any deeper insight or even a livelier interest in theological questions ; but it was the nature of the German to remain true to that which he had once received, and to preserve it unchanged. Thus the Germans conquerors were Arian, but the conquered Romans of the Western Empire were orthodox. Religious opposition was added to national opposition

This inner division weakened the noble kingdoms of the
Goths and of their kindred races.    One kingdom alone
had been orthodox from the first: the kingdom of
the Franks.    Clovis had embraced Christianity in the
Catholic form.    The Frankish conqueror professed the
same belief as the Roman population.    Nay, more, he
professed the same belief as the Roman provincials of
the Burgundian and West-Gothic kingdoms.    The
Roman noble, the Roman citizen, the Roman or
Catholic bishop in Southern Gaul, must have longed to
throw off the yoke of the hated Arian heretics, and
(since it could not be otherwise) chose rather to become
subject to the Catholic king of the Franks.    Clovis had
only to touch the kingdom of the West-Goths in Gaul
(in the battle of Vouglé, 506) and it fell into fragments.
The conquest of Burgundy was made under his sons;
the Burgundian kings had turned to Catholicism too
late.    Gaul, and with Gaul the heart of the Latin West,
became the possession of the Frankish conqueror.    It
was now only a question of time when the kingdom of
Clovis should be followed by that Empire which
encircled and formed anew the German-Roman world
—the Empire of Karl the Great.

## § 18. *Under the Merovingians*

Under the Merovingian kings in the sixth and
seventh centuries the culture of ancient Greece and
Rome made its voice last heard.    But the time was not
yet come for a new culture.    The world yet lived by
the last rays which the already sunken sun of ancient
culture still cast above the horizon.    There were schools
of rhetoric still in Southern Gaul which spread abroad

secular education, in direct continuation of the educational work of the ancient world. There was still a literature which followed closely the Roman models of the fifth century, and in form was a refinement on them. Even the Church was, in her place, the direct means of preserving the elements of culture inherited from the ancient Empire. Roman nationality, too, long held the foremost places among the clergy, and especially the bishops of the Church.

But the culture of the ancient world, by which the Merovingian age lived, was about to be extinguished. Its hour had come. The sixth century had still sufficient intellectual power to produce some literary works worthy of the remembrance of the historian. But already, when we look at Venantius Fortunatus, the greatest poet, and Gregory of Tours, the most important prose-writer of that age, we see that their language is already crude, their thought powerless. Bishop Gregory of Tours himself, by far the greater of the two writers named, with a nature full of noble simplicity, true grandeur of soul and manly strength, even he has but little wealth of intellect, refinement of culture, or gift of language ; he is already barbarized by contact with the coarser world which surrounds him.

The culture of the ancient world is coming to an end. In the seventh century it gives forth its last utterance, and at the beginning of the eighth its death-hour has struck. Its voice is silent. An age has come which no longer can give any account of itself. Culture no longer surrounds us, for the learning of the ancient world is dead, to be awakened to a new life only by the Carlovingian Renaissance.

What has been said of the history of learning in the Frankish kingdom holds good also of the history of the Church. The strength of the Church was extinguished under the Merovingians. In the sixth century, owing to that freedom which the German State brought as much to the individual as to the Church, there arose a Frankish Church, which was capable of a powerful development in various directions. But in the seventh century the Frankish Church was already overwhelmed by the weight of her temporal wealth and power. The bishop played the part of a great *Seigneur*, and placed himself at the head of the revolt of the aristocracy against the royal power. Spiritual interests fell into the background. Councils were hardly ever called. In the beginning of the eighth century there is a complete dissolution of the ecclesiastical body, so that in the time of the Empire's need, Karl Martell can do what he will with a Church from which the spirit is long fled, in order to re-establish the State by the help of the Church's possessions. Not far otherwise is the state of the Church in Italy, Spain, and Britain. In Italy the Church's life first suffered through the hatred of the Arian Lombards; then, after the conversion of the Lombards to Catholicism in the middle of the seventh century, through the ill-will of the Lombard kings, who remained in a state of natural feud with the Bishop of Rome. In Britain the Catholic and the Celtic forms of Christianity remained opposed (see page 86). In Spain, where Latin culture and ecclesiastical life were preserved in much greater energy than under the Frankish Empire, the Church immediately after the conversion of the West-Goths

to Catholicism in 587, became involved in quarrels
and intrigues, which, from the middle of the seventh
century, more and more undermined the royal throne
of the West-Goths.

The Church of the West stands in need of reform.
Who shall reform it? Can it turn to its natural lord,
the Bishop of Rome, as to its helper? Between
Greeks and Lombards, the Bishop of Rome himself
lies in sore need. Nay, more, the German kingdom,
the West-Gothic kingdom in Spain, the Frankish
kingdom in Gaul, and the kingdom of the Lombards
in Italy, cut off the Bishop of Rome from all direct
authority over the Church. Neither in the one kingdom nor the other can the German royal power
suffer the supreme authority of a foreign bishop. The
Church of the West is dissolved into national churches
—the Spanish, the Lombard, and the Frankish; and
the kings of the Anglo-Saxon kingdoms, which had
in like manner received their Christianity first from
Rome, claimed just the same sovereign power over
the English church as the Frankish king claimed
over the Frankish church. Western Christianity is
split up into many parts, and its ecclesiastical unity
is destroyed. The Bishop of Rome is divested of his
once supreme authority. The Papacy has no power
to ward off the impending destruction of the Church.
It lies itself overthrown, and waiting for its deliverer.
Who shall be the reformer of the Western Church?

## § 19. *The Frankish Reformation*

Germany in the sixth century was mainly heathen.
Although Alemanni, Bavarians, and Thuringians were

incorporated with the Frankish kingdom, with them Christianity was as yet in its infancy. The kingdom did not recognise it as its duty to make proselytes ; that was the business of the Church. But in the Frankish Church the want of living power was shown just in this inability to missionise. Not from the Franks, but from afar, from Ireland and from Scotland, after the end of the sixth century, came Celtic monks, speaking a strange language—greatest among them Columban (615) and Gallus (about 646)—that they might preach the Gospel to the Germans. They brought, with foreign ways and manners, a Christianity in many respects also foreign, and of a peculiarly Celtic stamp. In the first place, they reckoned Easter after a different fashion from that hitherto customary in the West ; besides this, the marriage of the priests was still valid among them. Above all, the regular episcopal constitution (hitherto the only form of ecclesiastical organization which held good everywhere) was unknown to them. The cloister was the centre alike of their mission and of their government ; and, side by side with the general spread of churches with an episcopal form of constitution, it seemed that Germany was to witness the rise of a monastic Church, organized after a Celtic model.

Thus the newly established German Church also brings about a new phase in the dissolution of Western Christendom.

At the beginning of the eighth century, the existence of the State itself was threatened in the West. First, the West-Gothic kingdom in Spain was overthrown by the Moors in 711 ; then the dukedom of Aquitaine (from the Pyrenees to the Loire) fell an easy prey to them. Already the foreign conquerors, filled with fanatical hatred, stood in the heart of the Frankish kingdom. At the same time the Slavic immigrants from the east were already pushing towards the Main and the Rhine. Where was the kingdom which should have granted protection? The kingdom of Clovis, that once mighty kingdom, had fallen. Its king was a mere boy of the Merovingian house. Alemanni, Bavarians, and Thuringians, under their several dukes, had renounced their allegiance to the sinking kingdom. Aquitaine also had revolted and formed an independent duchy, when it was reached and swallowed up by the Moorish invasion. In the rest of the kingdom anarchy ruled supreme. The great lords, the counts, dukes, the abbots and bishops, wrested the authority into their own hands. The kingdom became an empty name.

Not the Church alone, but Christianity was threatened. And, along with Christianity, the German nation.

At this critical moment, two men arose to be the saviours of the West; the one a political, the other an ecclesiastical reformer—Karl Martell and Boniface.

The battle of Poitiers (732), in which Karl Martell defeated the Arabs, was the sign of the approaching regeneration of the Empire. Upon the battle-field of Poitiers the Carlovingians made good their claim to the kingly and imperial crown.

The appearance of Boniface, a saint of the Catholic Church, in 719, as both a missionary from Germany and an ambassador of the Apostolic See, was the sign of the approaching regeneration of the Church.

Boniface, whose original name was Winfrid, was one of the Anglo-Saxon missionaries who had come over from England after the end of the seventh century, to convert the Germans. Gregory the Great (who was Pope from 590 to 604) had effected the conversion of the Anglo-Saxons directly through Rome, by sending the Benedictine monk Augustine to England. Augustine landed in England (597), spread abroad Christianity in Kent, and founded the Church of Canterbury, and with the Anglo-Saxons the Roman form of Christianity triumphed over the Celtic, after many battles. The Anglo-Saxon Church had paid back her debt to Rome. The Anglo-Saxon missionaries who came to Germany were preachers both of the Gospel and of the authority of the Roman See. It was in Rome that the Anglo-Saxon Willibrord received consecration as a bishop (695), in order to undertake his work as a missionary to the Frisians. It was from the Roman Bishop, Gregory II., that Boniface (Winfrid) sought his commission, when in the year 718 he conceived the full purpose of his work of mission. He came, not as the Celtic monk came, but to preach the Gospel to the Germans in the name of the Roman See. In the year 722 he was consecrated bishop in Rome, and at his consecration took the formal oath of obedience to the Bishop of Rome. And he was the first transalpine bishop who consented to do so. He believed with the full power of conviction that the salvation of the Church depended on Rome, and to this faith he had devoted his life. In this faith he conquered the West. He it is, and no other, who established the mediæval Papacy.

He was at once a missionary and a reformer. The Holy Oak at Geismar fell before his blows, a symbol of falling Paganism. He replaced the Celtic form of

Christianity by the Roman. He organized the regular episcopal constitution in Bavaria, and founded a number of new bishoprics in Hesse and Thuringia. His most important achievement was the reorganizing of the Frankish Church. After the death of Karl Martell (741), whose iron hand had lain heavy on the Frankish Church, and whose iron will was hostile to the reformation, he succeeded within a short time in reviving the regular forms of ecclesiastical constitution over the whole of the Frankish kingdom. Canon law was strictly enjoined, and the provincial synods of the bishops, with the metropolitans at their head, were restored as courts both of government and superintendence over all the bishops of the province. Before all, the Church of Gaul, like the Church of Germany, placed itself through Boniface in subjection to the Pope. The Pope was recognised as the supreme head of Western Christendom; his decisions were honoured with obedience; and the unity of the Western Church was thereby re-established.

The re-establishment of the Papal authority was the indispensable key-stone and corner-stone of the Frankish reformation. It had been shown that the dissolution of the Church into a number of national churches had not worked advantageously for the maintenance of the ecclesiastical system. One power there must be which would serve as a supreme authority, both to unite and to guide the whole Church. The power and full glory of the Church was necessary in order to make the power and glory of the Gospel sensibly visible to the people of the Middle Ages. Whatever served the power of the Church directly served the power of Christianity also. The special and necessary work of the Papacy was to make manifest the world-embracing organization of the Church, and at the same time to set forth the power of Christian ideas to govern the life of the mediæval nations. In establishing the power of the Roman See, Boniface in no way sold the German Church into slavery to Rome ; but he gave to it, as he gave to all Christendom, that decisive and fruitful touch of living power to which the glory of the Church, and with it the culture of the Middle Ages, owed its origin.

## § 20. *The Empire of Charles the Great*

The empire of Charles the Great was the completion of the kingdom founded by Clovis. The German and Roman races of the Western continent were now united in one supreme commonwealth. The mighty problem, the aim which ever hovered, now dim, now bright, before the Teutonic nations in their great migration, was solved at last. A new empire was established, as glorious, as powerful, as was once the Roman Empire of the West ; and when at Rome, on Christmas Day 800, Charles the Great received the imperial crown from the hands of the Roman people, and from the Bishop Leo III. as their head, he, as it were, gave utterance, with a conspicuous and imposing magnificence, to the living, joyous consciousness of his people, their consciousness that the great master-work had been accomplished, and that the lordship of the world had been given over to the Germans.

The new Roman Empire was to be at the same time a supreme Christian empire over the world. The Emperor appeared as the head of the State and the head of the Church. With this object, Charles the

Great first of all set aside the Bishop of Rome, and placed himself at the head of the government of the Church itself, presided at its councils, determined for bishops and abbots their spiritual rights, superintended every detail of church life, and with the help of his learned friend, the Anglo-Saxon Alcuin (died, abbot of Tours, 804), gave to it an impulse towards a richer, fresher life, by encouraging Latin culture and founding new places of education.

Charles the Great achieved his most important work for the Church by means of the Caroline Books (*Libri Carolini*), written by his order and published in his name. The Bishop of Rome decided in favour of the worship of images in the great controversy on the subject (see page 76). In the year 790 Pope Hadrian I. sent the decrees of the Nicene Synod of 787 (which had sanctioned image-worship) to Charles the Great, and through him to the Frankish Church, for promulgation. Charles the Great and his theologians answered the Pope's communication of the resolutions of an œcumenical council by an angry protest—the 'Caroline Books' (compiled between 790 and 794). In this 'work of the illustrious Charles, king of the Franks, against the foolish and presumptuous resolutions of a Greek synod in favour of image-worship' (so ran the official title), not only the worship, but the destruction of images was forbidden with genuine Christian determination and most admirable scholarship : images are indifferent in themselves ; no manner of worship is due to them, but also no manner of enmity. Let human art develop all its gifts in the service of God. The presence or absence of images in the churches has nothing to do with the essence of Christianity. Both the Greek Emperors with their iconoclasm, and the Greek Church with its worship of images, are in the wrong. The Pope also is in the wrong if he exacts from us subjection to the resolutions of the new Synod of Nicæa. The treatise was laid before the Synod of Frankfort (794); the assembled bishops of Gaul declared unanimously in its favour against the 'false Synod of the Greeks.' The King's book was delivered officially to Pope Hadrian. He answered by a decree, couched in terms of ironical suavity, in which, however, he laid stress on his determination to abide by the tradition of the Roman Church, and to damn all those who forbade the worship of images. Notwithstanding the Frankish Church remained true to its convictions throughout the ninth and tenth centuries, and not until the power of the Roman Church was strengthened in the course of the Middle Ages did the worship of images (which was maintained also by the Council of Trent) make its way into the Western Church. Up till that time the genius of Charles the Great (whose judgment on the question of image-worship was revived with a new power that bore fruit in life and art by the German Reformation) saved us from the invasion of Greek and Roman superstition.

Under Louis the Pious the great Empire crumbled away. In the person of Gregory IV. (833) the Papacy itself entered into an alliance with the sons of Louis the Pious to help in the destruction of the Empire—of the Empire which had made possible the establishment of Papal supremacy over the West. But with the unity of the Empire fell the supremacy of the Emperor which Charles the Great established over the Papacy, and, if the Church was to maintain its own unity, nothing else was left for it but to rely upon the authority of the Pope. The knowledge of this truth led to the publication, about the middle of the ninth century, of the 'Pseudo-Isidore, the work of a Gaulish divine, the most shameless, yet the most successful forgery of the Middle Ages. An old collection of Papal Decretals and Canons of Councils was increased by the addition of a large number of forged Decretals, which the author of the collection put forward under the names of the ancient bishops of Rome, of the second and third centuries, for the most part. The ever-recurring idea of the forgeries is, first, the freedom of bishops from temporal authority, nay, more, if possible, from every kind of accusation—none of the laity or of the inferior clergy may lay a charge or appear as a witness against a bishop; secondly, the subjection of the Church to the Pope. Another theory is also advanced: not only may every bishop, deposed by a provincial synod, have absolute right of appeal to Rome; according to the Pseudo-Isidore, the principle holds good universally, that all more important causes are to be laid before the Pope, and that no decision of a provincial synod is valid, unless confirmed by him. It was an unprecedented innovation in ecclesiastical law; law, the precise validity and authority of which were already established beyond a doubt. It was the programme of the Frankish party of reform which here received legal expression; the fate of the Church was to be dissevered from the fate of the perishing Empire, in order to found the Constitution of the Church, not only upon the Episcopate (freed from the authority of all local powers), but upon the Papacy. The unity of the Church was to be saved in spite of the dissolution of the Empire.

Hence the extraordinary success of the forgery. In the year 864, Pope Nicolas I. openly pronounced in favour of the principles laid down by the Pseudo-Isidore. He even went so far as to guarantee officially, although in ambiguous language, that the false Decretals (which, however, he took care not to mention by name) had been preserved in the archives of the Roman Church, and thus made the Papacy an accomplice in the deceit. By means of the false Decretals he defeated the most important, most learned, and most ambitious of the Frankish bishops, Hinkmar, Bishop of Rheims. The Pope, supported by the false Decretals, restored to his See, in 865, Rothad, Bishop of Soissons, whom Hinkmar had deposed. As early as the end of the ninth century, every objection against the genuineness of the false Decretals was silenced. They passed as genuine throughout the whole of the Middle Ages. They have been largely included in the *Corpus Juris Canonici*. No earlier than the fifteenth century, Cardinal Nicolas of Casa expressed a doubt of their genuineness, which, by the investigations of the Protestants (the Magdeburg Centuriators and others), was raised to a certainty. But meanwhile the false Decretals had done their work. Not that their work was to bring forth the mediæval Papacy—history is not to be deceived—but that they stood by the rising Papacy as its most powerful ally, in order to support its claims to ecclesiastical and temporal supremacy.

The Empire of Charles the Great had dissolved and fallen. If the unity of the Church was to be maintained, it could only be done by means of the Papacy. With the fall of the Carlovingian Empire, the foundations of mediæval Papal supremacy were laid.

And already the Papacy of the future was announced.
Nicolas I. (858-867) arose at that instant as one of its
most important representatives.   He subdued the
churches of the West Frankish kingdom, in the case
of Hinkmar.   He called to account King Lothar II.
for the divorce of his wife.   He reduced to subjection,
not only the King, but the Archbishops of Cologne
and Trèves, who had served him as abettors, together
with the whole Episcopate of Lotharingia.   He
even quarrelled with Photius, Patriarch of Constantinople, because he had refused to recognise the judgment of the Roman See, which declared not Photius,
but Ignatius, to be the legitimate Patriarch (863).
Nicolas and Photius mutually excommunicated and
deposed each other, even bringing questions of dogma
into the dispute ; and this was the occasion of the first
open rupture between the Latin and Greek Churches.
Nicolas proceeded to attack with equal vigour the
authority of the Metropolitans, the royal authority, and
his great rival at Constantinople.   The Papacy arose
to conquer the West, and to separate, as schismatic,
the refractory Greek communion from the body of the
true Church.

The Papacy entered on the inheritance of Charles the
Great.   On his way to world-wide supremacy, the
Bishop of Rome had only one more enemy to overcome
—the German Emperor.

# CHAPTER II

## THE GERMAN MIDDLE AGES

### § 21. *The German Emperors*

IT was Germany that first succeeded in bringing forth a new State. While France, Burgundy, and Italy were still in full process of dissolution, Henry I. laboured at that regeneration of Germany which was completed under his great son, Otho I. The victory which was won on the Lechfeld over the Hungarians in 955, revealed, both to the barbarous invaders and to all Europe, that in Germany a powerful State had been established. To the first power which arose on the ruins of the Carlovingian Empire there fell naturally the imperial crown, and, with it, that supremacy over Italy which was to bring with it a curse as well as a blessing. In the year 962, Otho the Great was crowned Roman Emperor by the Pope. The crown of Charles the Great had again an heir who was in a position to make the imperial power felt. Yet, nevertheless, the political situation was altogether different under Otho from what it was under Charles the Great.

To Otho the Great belonged only a portion of the former kingdom of the Franks: the kingdom of the East Franks (Ostarrihhi) on the Rhine, the Elbe, the Main, and the Danube, to which was now added Italy.

According to the political doctrine of the Middle Ages, the world, at any rate the Western world, was to be subject to the imperial authority. But the supremacy of the German Emperor remained a mere name to countries outside Germany. It meant in point of fact only that supremacy over Italy, so often fought for and so fatal when won. And in Germany itself the royal power, upon which, nevertheless, the imperial authority rested, fell far short of the position formerly assumed by the Frankish kings. The Feudal System had arisen in the meanwhile, and had changed the constitution of the State. The Count was no longer, as before, the official organ of the royal will, but a vassal whose county belonged to him as a fief in his own right. Moreover, above the Count the great duchies had arisen, the Swabian, the Bavarian, the Frankish, the Lotharingian and the Saxon, which possessed a power altogether equal to that of the King. The royal power was in danger of being turned from a real supremacy into a mere feudal over-lordship. Otho the Great saved it from this danger by two measures. First, he attached the duchies as much as possible to his own family, and thus turned the resources of the duchy into resources of the kingdom. This measure was only partially successful; since his own brother, the Duke of Bavaria, and his own son, the Duke of Swabia, were far more inclined to rebel against the royal power than to be obedient to it. The decisive measure, which Otho the Great employed, was to build the new kingdom on the power of the Church. Under him, it became an express principle of the royal policy to raise the power of the Church, especially of the bishops, by enriching them with gifts, bestowing on them public privileges, and even making them Counts. And wherefore? In order that the power of the spiritual princes might counterbalance that of the arrogant temporal princes. The King was surer of the spiritual lords than he was of the temporal. The King himself nominated the bishop and abbot of the imperial monasteries by means of the investiture with ring and crosier. He was more free to nominate the bishop and abbot than the count and duke, because spiritual offices were not hereditary, neither could be hereditary. The spiritual dignities in every case of death fell again into the King's hands at his disposal, and could always be filled by the persons most agreeable to the King.

Even property belonging to the spiritual foundations passed as in some measure the property of the Empire. What the spiritual foundation gained was not therefore lost to the Empire. On the contrary, it became rather the more certain possession of the Empire, by being withdrawn from the hands of the great temporal vassals. The King received subsidies, under the name of gifts, from the Church-lands, and from Church-lands the greater part of his troops was supplied in case of war. So over Church-lands the King set up the bishop or the abbot most agreeable to him. Thus the German Kingdom and the German Empire of the Middle Ages became possible. Its supremacy found a material substratum in the power of the Church; and the royal investiture represented the means by which the Church was bound to the King.

It was a kingdom built upon a broad foundation. But would not that foundation itself begin to tremble in the moment when the Church, by reason of its spiritual nature, desired freedom from the authority of the State?

From the time of the dissolution of the Carlovingian Empire the Papacy had also gone through a period of decline, though it succeeded in exercising its power in isolated instances; but in the main the national Churches of Germany, France, and England governed themselves. The age of national Churches was apparently renewed. But it was with the Emperor that there lay that determining force which now once more saved the Church from dissolution. According to the belief of the Middle Ages, the Emperor also was possessed of peculiar spiritual virtue, and the German Synods, over which he presided in the tenth and eleventh centuries, were at the same time representative of the entire Church. Above all, the Emperor, as the head of all Christendom, was not only justified in exalting the Papacy, but bound to do so. The Papacy, as it existed at the end of the ninth and beginning of the tenth centuries, was laid low by the violence of the civic aristocracy, and the very scum of a rude society disgraced the Papal throne. The Roman Papacy had to be delivered from the Romans. Otho the Great, his son, and his grandson, interposed repeatedly. The Romans had taken oath to Otho, to elect no Pope without his confirmation. Many a time the Emperor interfered in order that through his influence on the nomination he might bring new life to the Papacy; but for the most part his interference was in vain. In the first half of the eleventh century the great hereditary nobility of Rome, the Crescentii and the Tusculans, fought for the Papal power as for a family possession. In the year 1033, Benedict IX., a boy of twelve years, was actually raised to the Papal See, which he afterwards stained with all manner of vice. By a popular insurrection he was driven from the city, in 1044, in order that Sylvester III. might be raised to the Papacy as his rival. When, notwithstanding, Benedict IX. returned to Rome with an armed force, he sold his Papacy to Gregory VI.; but without any idea of giving up the papal authority. The scandal had reached its height. The German Emperor appeared as the only power that could give help. Henry III. interposed, and, under his powerful protection, the Synod of Sutri (1046) deposed the two rival Popes, and later, the Synod of Rome (December 1046) deposed Benedict IX. also. A German bishop, Suidger of Bamberg, was elected Pope in Rome under the name of Clement II. (1046-1049). He placed the imperial crown on the head of Henry III. At the same time the Emperor received the rank and authority of a Roman patrician, together with the right of nomination to the Roman See. From that day the nomination of the Popes became a recognised function of the German government.

Three more Popes were nominated by Henry III.: Damasus II. (1047); Leo IX. (1048-1054, a native of Alsace, of the family of the Counts of Dachsburg, elected at the Diet of Worms); and Victor II. (1054-1057, elected at the Diet of Mainz). The Pope was elected no longer in Rome, but in Germany.

The Emperor was at the height of his power. The German Church was bound to his service. Even the united Church of the Empire recognised in him, as in the days of Charles the Great, its superior ruler, in that the appointment to the highest spiritual dignities belonged to him.

But it was only for a moment that the ecclesiastical

movement favoured the authority of the Emperor. For that moment no other means was at hand to help the Papacy and the Church out of their difficulty, save the powerful aid of the Emperor. But this solution of the problem could not be regarded as a final disposal of the question of reform. The protection of the Emperor was altogether inadequate. As long as the arm of the Emperor was dreaded, so long the protection which it lent was effectual. But as soon as the direct pressure of the imperial authority was relaxed—and the Emperor was too often at a distance and occupied with other cares—then the Papacy fell again a prey to the petty tyrants of Rome. The Church required the establishment of the Papacy in its own might, and this the Emperor was unable to ensure. The help of the Emperor was accepted for the moment. But when the Papacy was successfully re-established as a power capable of independent action, then its determined aim would necessarily be the deliverance, not only of the Pope, but of the Church, from the authority of the Emperor. Once the Church and the Papacy were truly *reformed* (in the ecclesiastical sense) by the help of the Emperor, then had the hour struck for the formation of the Pope's supremacy.

## § 22. *Reform of Monasticism*

While the world was full of the fame of men like Otho and Henry, a spiritual movement had already begun in the quiet cells of the cloister which was destined to transform the Empire and the Papacy.

The learning of the tenth and the eleventh centuries was the fruit of the Carlovingian Renaissance, of the

Carlovingian revival of Latin culture.   It was the age
of Roman architecture, that style in which the spirit of
Christianity was united with classic form.   Like its
churches and its imperial palaces, the entire culture of
that age was Roman in its style.   Virgil was the poet
most honoured in that period.   Latin was the language
not only of the clergy, but of the higher classes generally.
It was the age in which the Latin comedies of the nun
Hroswitha were represented before a public of illustrious
ladies ; in which the monk Ekkehard (I.) translated the
*Waltharilied* into Latin verse, and so into the form of
the literature of the Court, in which even the naïve songs
of the people occasionally found utterance in the Latin
tongue.   Besides the Court of the Emperor, other
centres and representatives of that Virgilian culture
were the monasteries, which we may call the Universities
of that age—the most important of the German cloisters
being the monastery of St. Gallen, renowned far and
wide for its scholars and artists.   The part of leader in
the development of intellectual life which later was
taken by the royal Court and afterwards (from the
sixteenth century) by the cities, belonged at that time
to the Court of the Emperor and to the cloisters.
Thence the intellectual impulses which moved the
educated world took their rise.   There was no interest,
either of art or science, or even, we may say, of popular
and political life, which lay beyond the reach of these
monkish professors.   There was no power which was
not thought worthy of being used, no faculty which did
not find a school there to train it to masterly perfection.
The watchword of these monasteries and nunneries was
not the annihilation but the fulfilment of individuality.
It meant to have an ear, not only for psalmody but for

the music of the heroic songs of Germany; to have an eye not only for letters, the rudiments of learning, but for painting, with the splendour of its sensuous charm, that looked not only to art but to nature; nay, more, it meant to have a heart, not only for the Latin of Virgil, but for our wonderful, scarce discovered German mother-tongue, which became, as it were, for the first time conscious of its power within the cloistral walls of St. Gallen. It was a monasticism which stood in the mid-stream of the national life, ready both to give and to receive, and ruled the world of that time by sheer force of intellect.

But was it then the aim of Monasticism to rule the world, to enjoy its good things, and to share the life of the nation? Was not its ideal rather to forsake the world, to despise its noblest possessions as nought, and as unworthy of the immortal soul—nay, more, as a danger in themselves, as a part of that world which is synonymous with evil, with sin, and corruption?

The annihilation, the mortification, not only of evil affections, but of *all* earthward impulses of man; not the completion, but the destruction of the earthly gifts pertaining to the person;—that is the characteristic and native watchword of Monasticism. And the monks of St. Gallen, and of all other Benedictine Monasteries in Germany and France, were fallen very far from that ideal. There could be no doubt that not only a sense for all that was noble and great in that age, but that worldly sense of the lowest kind, had found its way into the cloisters. Monastic disciples declined; there was no longer any question of superintendence over the individual. The Abbot himself might be one of the culprits. The more the national spirit, the devotion to a life of culture in general, obtained the upper hand in the cloisters, the more did ancient Monasticism, with its rigour and self-torture, tend to disappear. A voluptuous and licentious mode of life appeared in the cloisters ; cloistral seclusion ceased to be the rule ; the seats of asceticism were turned into halls of luxury. The interests of asceticism withdrew before the interest of culture. It was evident that this state of things struck at the very roots of the genuine monastic life. From the purely monastic standpoint, the salt of Monasticism had lost its savour. Therefore Monasticism of this Roman and Virgilian type, the Monasticism of Ekkehard, was to be cast forth and trodden under foot of men. It was the cloister of Cluny, founded on Burgundian soil, close to the French border, that pronounced judgment on a Monasticism so fallen from its own ideal. Here, as early as in the tenth century, the old rule of the Benedictines was renewed and sharpened by the Abbot Odo (927-941). It sought to check every earthward tendency by means of a rigorous rule, which went into the minutest details. The introduction of a rule of silence in certain places and at certain times was to be a means at once of obtaining complete mastery over self and of skilfully stimulating the inner and spiritual life. In the monks of Cluny there arose anew the old monastic ideal of renunciation, and of the torture of the flesh, in opposition to the degenerate Monasticism of the West. And as this ideal became visible, it was bound to win over to its side the world of the Middle Ages. These monks of Cluny with their mortified bodies, with their glowing eyes and haggard faces, became the saints of the people ;

for in them the Christian ideal, as conceived by the Middle Ages, had become again alive. The peasant sunk in coarsest sensuality saw here, in bodily form before his eyes, the spirit of Christianity which triumphantly overcomes this world of earth. The Monasticism of Cluny became the centre of a powerful and enthusiastic movement. Numerous cloisters united themselves with the mother-cloister of Cluny in one congregation, under the single government and superintendence of the Abbot of Cluny. The reformation was at the same time a reorganisation of Monasticism. The old confusion, which prevailed so long as every cloister was independently governed under its own abbot, was done away with by the one uniform constitution through which the power over a strong and widely extended union of monastic institutions was committed to a single superintendent-general. The Abbot of Cluny, the first General of the Order, received the title of Arch-Abbot. The movement had arisen on Roman soil, and there it produced its first great effect. But even in the eleventh century it ruled the West. The German Emperors themselves looked favourably on the cause of reform, and lent their help to change one cloister after another (including even the famous monastery of St. Gallen) from the old traditional fashion to the new and vigorous ' Italian ' form. In this new-born Monasticism there lay the force which gave to the Church a new inner life, which won over large classes of the population to the Church's ideal, which delivered the Church from her subordination to the temporal power, and brought forth the age of the mediæval hierarchy. It was from the cloister-cell that the world of the Middle Ages arose, and from the cloister-cell its destruction afterwards went forth in the person of Martin Luther.

The fate of the future was already decided when, in Germany also, the Emperor Henry III. put forth all his power to open the way for the reforms of Cluny; and later, in the person of Gregory VII. (the monk Hildebrand), the Monasticism of Cluny ascended the papal throne.

### § 23. *Ecclesiastical Reform*

The ideals of Cluny were by no means limited to the reform of Monasticism. Ecclesiastical and monastic reform were rather to proceed hand in hand. The aim was to deliver from the world not only the monasteries, but the Church. There were two ways toward the deliverance of the Church, and both ways were taken.

One way was the renunciation of the world on the part of the Church; renunciation of its revenues, its wealth, its dignities, its principalities, its privileges of rule and all its glory. In consideration of her renunciation of all temporal power, the Church could then with right and justice insist on her deliverance from the temporal authority, more particularly on her deliverance from investiture at the hands of the laity. This was felt to be a means of secularisation of the Church, especially through the simony, that is, the sale of ecclesiastical offices, which in many ways it actually involved. This ideal of poverty was the pure and natural result of the ideas of Cluny. It meant that monastic poverty and renunciation were to be binding upon the Church in general. From this ideal of poverty there followed, as its consequence, the idea which arose equally in Cluny, of a celibate priesthood:

renunciation of the world includes the renunciation of marriage. With the Church, as with the monastery, it was a question of realizing the imitation of Christ, as conceived by the Middle Ages, with regard not only to their renunciation of all possessions, but to the celibacy of the whole body of the clergy; in a word, it was a question of monasticizing the secular clergy.

The other way was to lay foundations for the Church's supremacy over the world. The Church could also become free from the world by subduing the world. Here again this method demanded the abrogation of investiture by the laity; but the State was by no means to take back from the Church her worldly possessions. Rather, the Church was to cling to all her temporal wealth and power with a firm hand, while she demanded that her worldly possessions should be freed from the authority of the State. The Church claimed the world for her own, and required the State to give her room—that she might assume the position of a State. The supremacy of ecclesiastical authority over that of the State, even in temporal affairs, was here the leading thought. As the ideal of poverty sprang from the opinions of the monastic clergy, so that of supremacy arose from the instinct of the episcopal—the secular—clergy.

When, towards the middle of the eleventh century, the Cluniac movement gained hold on the people in the towns of Upper Italy (beginning with Milan in 1056), and roused the 'pataria,' or rabble, to revolt against the wealthy and luxurious secular clergy who were the ruling class, it was the monastic ideal of poverty which governed the course of reform and stirred up the masses of the citizens to protest, not only against the wealth and temporal government of the priests, but against their marriage. And this ideal of poverty never wholly died out in the Church ; it was realised later, in a more legitimately ecclesiastical form, by the Mendicant Orders. But its complete realization was hindered by the insurmountable opposition of the secular clergy. When, in the year 1111, Pope Paschal II. was willing to buy the Church's freedom from the lay investiture at the price of her renunciation of all her possessions and rights of government, there arose from the ranks of the clergy a storm of opposition to which the Pope himself was compelled to yield. But the point of celibacy was carried through, especially as it was subservient, not only to the ideal of poverty, but to the power of the Church ; inasmuch as by freeing the priest from all family ties it made him the dependant and servant of the Church alone. So far the monastic ideal conquered. But there was no renunciation of temporal power and authority. The interests of the secular clergy, that is, of the Episcopate, were here stronger than the purely ideal interests of the Church.

The question was decided for the Church by the powerful Gregory VII., who was not only a bishop but a monk. As a monk he forbade the marriage of the clergy ; as a bishop the influence of temporal glory was too strong for him. Through him the mediæval ideal of ecclesiastical supremacy attained, so to speak, self-consciousness ; through him it was proclaimed with a mighty voice, and realized with all the unhesitating energy of a ruling spirit, whose genius was far above that of any of his contemporaries. It was he who instituted, in 1074, the law of celibacy, by which every married priest was forbidden to serve at the holy altar

on pain of excommunication. It was he also who
instituted, in 1075, the law against investiture, by which
the German king, Henry IV., was refused the right of
investiture with ring and crosier, that is, the right to
make grants of the bishoprics and abbeys of his
kingdom. When he determined to build upon the
foundations of the intellectual movement which had
its beginning in Cluny, and had developed in the meanwhile, he made it possible to fling down the gauntlet to
the German Empire, which under Henry III. was too
strong for the Papacy. His strong confidence was
justified by the course of history. When, in 1076,
Gregory VII. thundered forth his anathemas against
Henry IV., the German king had to exchange his royal
mantle for the sackcloth of penance, and to go down on
his knees in the snow of winter, before the gates of the
Castle of Canossa, and thus in an ignoble humiliation,
which was a shame both to himself and to his rival, to
crave absolution from the haughty priest. The high
tide of ecclesiastical thought was too strong for the
loose fabric of the mediæval State. And just as this
powerful Pope established his supremacy over the
German throne by the raising and deposing of rival
kings, so by his gift of Apulia and Calabria to the
Norman Duke, Robert Guiscard ; by the help he gave
to William the Conqueror in his invasion of England ;
by his interference in the struggles for the crown in
Hungary, Poland, and Dalmatia ; by his opposition to
the Spanish Courts and the Princes of Sardinia, he
realized in all parts of the Western world the idea to
which he had devoted his life—the idea of the Supremacy
of the Church. And at his death, even in his exile,
fleeing before Henry IV., a prisoner rather than a

comrade of the Normans by whom he was surrounded, the legacy which he left to his posterity was the establishment of the Church as God's own State supreme over the world.

And thus upon the supremacy of the Empire there followed directly the age of Papal supremacy.

## § 24. *The Concordat of Worms*

Certainly Gregory VII.'s ideal of Papal supremacy never was nor could be fully realized. That was plainly shown in the dispute about the investiture. In the year 1122, that conflict was formally ended for Germany, by the Concordat of Worms, concluded between the Emperor Henry V. and Pope Calixtus II. By this treaty the symbols of investiture were changed; the Emperor was to invest no longer with the ring and crosier, but with the sceptre. This expressly signified that the temporal possessions of the Church were alone the object of imperial investiture: the bishop or abbot who was elected received only the 'regalia,' and not his spiritual office, by royal investiture. Nay, more, the Emperor's free right of nomination was expressly done away with, and the Emperor gave his sanction to Canonical election by the community, under the leadership of the clergy and of the nobility, especially the brethren of the monasteries. But the presence of the Emperor, or of his legate, at the election, and his right to a decision in concert with the provincial synods in the case of a disputed election, gave him, as before, the casting vote in the appointment of bishoprics and imperial abbeys. The more so, because, according to the Concordat, the elected candidates were invested

before the rite of consecration. If the Emperor refused
the investiture, in point of fact the rite of consecration
(which, for instance, made a bishop or an abbot) could
not be completed. It was altogether impossible that
any person not approved of by the Emperor could
attain the position of bishop or abbot. In the course
of the twelfth century, and later, the German Emperors
repeatedly renounced their right of investiture before
consecration. But in spite of this fact the right remained, and was exercised. Nay, more, in those cases
where the investiture was only performed after the
consecration (and by the Concordat itself this was
made the rule from the very first, for foreign countries
lying within the German Empire, such as Burgundy
and Italy), as long as full investiture represented a free
right of the Emperor, so long there remained ensured
to him an influence on the election. No person could
very well be elected and consecrated when it was
certain that he would not receive the investiture. Thus
by the Concordat of Worms the imperial investiture
was changed only in form. The case remained the
same as before. The more so, because, according to
the express wording of the Concordat, all that the
bishoprics and imperial abbeys owed to the Empire in
the supplying of troops and the payment of dues remained unchanged. It was impossible for the Emperor
to relinquish his hold on the spiritual principalities ;
for the good reason, that in doing so he would have
given up the foundations of his own power. The agreement made as to the imperial investiture meant that the
Empire asserted itself as a living power independent of
the Church. It triumphantly repelled the Church's
attack upon the temporal conditions of its existence.

During the whole of the twelfth, during the whole of the thirteenth century, up to the time of the inter-regnum, the German Emperors' right of investiture remained the most important source of the imperial authority ; and the splendour of the imperial house of Hohenstaufen, as once that of Otho's line, was owing in the first place to the power which the German Emperor exercised over the German Church and its possessions. When, during the interregnum and after it, the German kingdom was completely dissolved, and the duties which the spiritual princes owed to the Empire also ceased, then for the first time the right of royal investiture lost its meaning.  It became a mere form.  The knights (who represented the community, and as late as the twelfth century shared with the clergy in the election of bishops) at this time withdrew from the election. Nay, more, the greater part even of the clergy must have voluntarily relinquished their right in it.  For most of the dioceses the cathedral chapter assumed the position of the sole legitimate elective body, a body exclusively and purely ecclesiastical, which still less admitted the claims of the political authority.  The investiture of bishops and of the imperial abbots likewise became a mere form, just like that of the great temporal vassals. Instead of the Emperor, the Pope now acquired the decisive influence.  Not the Concordat of Worms, but the victorious revolt of the princely nobility against the declining Emperors, together with the rising power of the cathedral chapter, which began at the time of the interregnum, first deprived the Emperor's function of investiture of the meaning which it once possessed.

In the eleventh and twelfth centuries the Emperor asserted himself against the theories of Gregory, and

would not suffer the Empire to be degraded to a mere
empire of priests. Throughout the West the Pope
experienced the same opposition as in Germany. The
right of appointment to ecclesiastical offices, which
albeit in a different form belongs to the State up to the
present day, represents, in spite of all instances to the
contrary, the result of that royal function of investiture
which not only in Germany, but in France, in England,
and in the whole circle of the mediæval Roman-German
State generally, was once the offspring of mediæval law.

## § 25. *The Crusades and Chivalry*

The Church was not able to put the State altogether
aside. However, under Gregory VII. and his followers,
she obtained the upper hand. Like an overpowering
wave the claims of the Church and of religion arose and
gathered to themselves all the culture and education of
the Middle Ages. In the course of the eleventh century
pilgrimages to the Holy Land became even greater and
more frequent. With all the rudeness and sensual
power of that age, the question 'What must I do to be
saved?' became, notwithstanding, the ruling question ;
and man's inborn longing after the heavenly Jerusalem
found utterance, in its mediæval form, in the yearning
of the Western world to behold the earthly Jerusalem.
On this account, towards the end of the eleventh
century, the outcry of the returning pilgrims against
the outrages of the Saracens aroused a mighty answer
over the whole West. But it was neither emperor nor
king, but a pope, Urban II., who aroused all Christendom
to arms at the Council of Clermont in 1095. The result
was astounding. The Crusades were the greatest

military undertaking which the Middle Ages had seen. The whole manly force of Western chivalry now arose, once for all, to repel the attack of Mohammedanism upon Christianity with a mightier attack. Throughout two centuries, the idea of the deliverance of the Holy Sepulchre continued to be the supreme interest of Europe ; again and again did emperor and kings stir up anew the flower of the knighthood of Europe to crusades in the far-off Holy Land, which was lit by the sun of the East and by the splendour of Christian history—the history of salvation. The military service which was rendered to God and to Christ was at the same time a campaign in the service of the Church and of its head. The Crusades, for which the chivalry of the West drew the sword again and again, meant in point of fact that the Pope was the greatest, the mightiest, and highest military sovereign of the West.

The chivalry of the West rested on a single international idea : it represented, in the imagination of the Middle Ages, one great united society, not divided by boundaries of country and government,—a society into which the young noble was received by proof of arms and by laying on of knighthood. All the great products of the Middle Ages bear this character of universality. As was the Church, the Empire, and the scholastic culture of the Middle Ages, such was the organization of the mediæval nobility. The universal Empire of Rome finds its mediæval reflection in the culture of chivalry too. The Christian nobility, that is to say, a nobility not French or German, but simply Christian, represented the armed knighthood of the Empire, and this was now pre-eminently a Church.

The head of all knights was the Emperor, the supreme

temporal head of Christendom, that is, of the Empire
But it was his glory and his pride, together with the
united chivalry of the Church, to serve the Pope.
Knighthood was a society which represented at once
the interests of the nobility and of the clergy. Scarcely
had the movement of the Crusades begun at the end of
the eleventh century, when, at the beginning of the
twelfth, the great Orders were founded ; that of the
Knights Templar in 1119 ; that of the Knights of St.
John in 1120. The Orders assumed a spiritual organization, that they might perform the service which they
owed to the Church. The monk drew his sword in
order to fulfil at once his monastic and his knightly
vows. And these proud Orders of Knights, which
embraced the whole extent of Christendom, recognized
but one sovereign—the Pope. A standing army of
knights who were monks was at the disposal of the
Pope, loosening the bonds of the temporal States (which
had the local command of the Orders), and at the same
time plainly revealing with how strong a hand the
Church was now able to wield the temporal sword.

This movement against the East, a movement half
spiritual, half military, helped to complete the supremacy of the Pope over the West. The day came when,
at the Pope's command, a crusade was started in the
north of France to wipe out in blood the heresy of the
Albigenses (the Catharists or *Cathari*) of the South
(1209) ; when King John of England received his kingdom as a gift from the Pope (1213) ; when the strife
between the knights of Livonia and the bishop of Riga
over Livonia and Esthonia, newly won to Christendom,
was referred to the Pope, as if these lands had been
the peculiar possession of St. Peter (1210) ; when the

Knights of Germany received Culm and Prussia as a gift from St. Peter (1226); and when, by means of a sudden crusade, a Latin Empire and a Latin Church dependent on Rome were erected in Constantinople (1204). The Papacy had become the foremost political power. And this was the more marvellous seeing that it was dependent for this its worldly power on those very monks who had forsworn the world.


### § 26. *Monasticism—The Mendicant Orders*

The monks had drawn the sword. At the same time they arose with ever renewed endeavour to realize, before all, the spiritual ideals of Monasticism, the ideals of Catholic Christendom. The highest aim of mediæval and of modern Catholic piety is, for the individual, asceticism, the striving after renunciation of the world and all it has to offer. The ideal of mediæval and of Catholic Christendom is the monk who escapes from the world into the cloister-cell, that there he may crucify his flesh with all its affections. Yet the world pursued the monk into the cloister, and he could not escape from it. Wealth and power, the interests of politics and of culture, had laid hold on the monks of the Merovingians and Otho's time, and estranged them from their original purpose. The monks of Cluny represented in the tenth and eleventh centuries the first great returning tide of the true monastic spirit. But it was in the twelfth century that the spirit of asceticism first attained its full motive power. Monasticism was revived in a succession of new forms, each in its different way expressing the action of the ascetic idea: the Orders of the Carthusians, the

Premonstrants, the Carmelites, etc.  In this movement
the Cistercian monks, and especially their great Abbot,
Bernard of Clairvaux, played the chief part, which was
afterwards taken by the Order of Mendicants.

The first half of the twelfth century was the age of
Bernard of Clairvaux (1091-1153).  By his word alone
he ruled the world, with its Popes, Emperor, and Kings.
He decided between the claims of Pope Innocent II.
and his rival Anacletus II., and laid the West in
subjection to Innocent.  By the power of his oratory
he urged the Emperor Conrad III. to the second great
Crusade (1147).  Pope Eugenius III. (1145-1153), a
Cistercian monk and pupil of Bernard's, was a tool in
his hands.  But this man, who compelled the world to
bow before the sovereign power of his intellect, found
satisfaction for his own innermost being only when he
forsook all worldly things, that, in the midst of solitude,
he might live for the contemplation of the Divine love,
and for the rapture of communion with the Almighty
alone.  As Augustine was the father of Western
theology, Bernard was the father of Western mysticism.
The ardour of his spiritual emotion burst forth from his
innermost soul in immortal songs.  His *Salve caput
cruentatum*, which Paul Gerhardt has paraphrased in
his hymn 'O Sacred Head, with blood and wounds,'
etc., peals like the music of an organ, uniting the power
of its sublime subject with the natural force of perfect
religious fervour and of a poetic genius of unearthly
splendour.  Urged by his longing after God, while he
was a young man belonging to a noble family of
Burgundy, he avoided the already wealthy Order of
Cluny, and entered an Order newly founded, poor and
insignificant, which had sprung up in the depths of the

forest of Citeaux, near Dijon—the Order of Cistercians. He made the greatness and the power of his Order. In two years' time, in order to accommodate the increasing numbers of members, a larger monastery had to be built at Clairvaux, situated in a wild solitude; and Bernard was chosen for its Abbot. Numbers of other monasteries were afterwards founded over the whole extent of the West. Up to the middle of the thirteenth century the Order of Cistercians (or of Bernardines) was the leading Monastic Order. He erected his monasteries, which in their architecture were fore-runners of the new and aspiring Gothic style, in some waste desert place, or in the heart of the silent primæval forest, that they might be homes of Christian life and of industry alike. The Cistercian monasteries were in the Middle Ages the pioneers not only of Monasticism but of agricultural labour, which pressed on courageously into the wilderness of yet untamed nature, and cast the charm of a kindlier grace over the dumb landscape of primæval time. In East Germany these cloisters were centres not only for the conversion of the heathen, but for the spread of agriculture and German civilisation. What a fulness of life to be set free by a single man!

The Middle Ages produced yet another spiritual creative genius, of even more supreme importance than Bernard of Clairvaux—Francis of Assisi (born 1182). In this strange man the power of faith brought forth its fairest fruit, the power of love. Following the example of his Lord and Master, his own desire was to give all that he had to the poor, and to preach the gospel of repentance and of love. He did this, and more; he succeeded in making others do the same. From his work of practical Christianity (as he understood it in

a monastic and ascetic sense) made perfect by the power
of an unconquerable love, there arose the Mendicant
Orders, and these Orders, especially the Franciscans
(founded 1209) and the Dominicans (founded 1215),
ruled the whole course of the history of the Western
Church during the second half of the Middle Ages.

Francis of Assisi, from whom the Franciscans
received their name, undertook to realise the ideal of
poverty, not only for the individual monk, but for the
entire community of the cloisters and the Orders.
Even the monastic community itself, that is, the Cloister,
or the Order, was to be incapable of possessing property,
in order that wealth (the constant enemy of cloistral
rule) might be excluded, and that the brethren might
be beggars, abandoned to necessity and poverty, thrown
back for their support upon the charitable gifts which
they begged; so might they learn with humility and
renunciation to lead a life devoted to love alone and
the service of others. Such was the power of ascetic
resolution. It had a widespread influence, because it
gave the fullest expression to the ideals of mediæval
piety, though it could not always be more than very
partially carried out. From the very first there
appeared within the Franciscan Order a milder
tendency, which aimed at the acquisition of property,
art, and knowledge, in opposition to the rigour of its
founder. The Dominican Order followed the example
of the Franciscans, only with certain reservations and
limitations. But enough of the original idea remained
to conquer the Middle Ages. The Mendicant Orders
had no need to support their members; they lived upon
the alms of the faithful. Thus they had no need to
limit the number of members they admitted. The

principle of mendicancy further involved the abrogation of the old monastic system of seclusion. The band of mendicant monks streamed forth far and wide over the whole land, that they might carry everywhere, along with their request for charity, the spirit, the doctrine, and the convictions of Monasticism. The mendicant monks soon became the confessors, pastors, and preachers most beloved by the people. Freed from episcopal authority by papal privileges, in order that they might be in direct subjection to the Pope, they were untrammelled by the authority either of the bishop or the parish priest. To them all Christendom was one single community, open to their impressive preaching, which worked upon the masses, touching every interest, political, ecclesiastical, and spiritual, in equal degree. The founder of the Franciscan Order even undertook to cast, as it were, the net of his rule directly over the whole world. He created the 'Third Order' of Saint Francis, the members of which were known as 'Tertiaries,' both men and women, and gave to the laity also a monastic character. The Tertiary remained in the world, in the married state, or in his profession ; but in other respects he took upon himself all the puritan rigour of monastic life, with the renunciation even of those joys of life hitherto permitted, and bound himself by an oath to the practice of the most earnest morality. A grey frock, with a cord for girdle, gave him even the outward appearance of an ascetic. As the reformers of Cluny had set themselves to monasticize the secular clergy in earlier time, so now the attempt was made in still grander fashion to monasticize the laity itself. If monasticism be indeed the true and proper calling of a Christian, then of every

Christian it must be required as an ideal that he renounce the world and devote himself by a monastic life to God and to Christ alone.  If Monasticism is the truth, Monasticism must desire to draw all Christendom after it into the cloister.  This attempt was made by Francis of Assisi, so far as it was practicable. Monasticism was conceived to be the form of Christian life which was valid for all.  As the monks had once forsaken the Church, they now turned back to the Church in order to transform it after their own fashion. In this moment the principle of mediæval Catholicism celebrated its highest triumph.  The power which strove to merit salvation by the works of the law, by mortification of the flesh and renunciation of the world, filled the Church and ruled the world far and wide.

We must consider further that the Mendicant Orders, especially the Dominicans, were soon rapidly rising to power, and held their own interests to be identical with those of the Papacy.  The Pope delivered them from the episcopal authority.  By means of the privileges he granted to them he opened out a free path for their unhindered activity.  Thus the strengthening of the papal authority which served the Order as a protection against the authority of their regular ecclesiastical superiors, was the direct interest of the Order itself. In all parts of the Church, the Mendicant monks with their privileges were a living witness to the far-reaching authority of the Papacy ; and as the power of the regular temporal authority, of Emperor, Kings, and Princes, was injured by the direct subordination to the Pope of the Orders of Knights, so the regular spiritual authority of bishops and archbishops was maimed by the similar subordination of the Mendicant Orders.

The authority of the Papacy was everywhere supreme, and threatened with danger the whole traditional order both of Church and State.

We must still further consider that it was directly by means of the Mendicant Orders, more particularly of the Dominicans, that, from the thirteenth century onwards, preaching acquired a steadily increasing importance in the life of the people. Hitherto divine service had consisted principally of worship. The parish priest, and even the bishop, were seldom qualified to deliver spiritual discourse. Divine service was for the most part speechless. The solemnities of the mass, the splendid vestments, the mysterious ceremonial alone, aroused religious awe in a congregation which was more a spectator of the service than a partaker therein. The aim of divine worship, and its crowning glory, was that feeling of the immediate omnipresence of the Divine Man which constrained the congregation to bow down in adoration ; and this feeling nourished not only faith but manifold superstitions. By means of the Mendicants the eloquence of spiritual discourse first developed its full powers amongst the assembled people. Yet the sermon still remained no regular part of divine service. But it had appeared on the field, it made a place for preaching beside the sacraments, and it was a preparation for the age of the sixteenth century, when the great reformation of the Church was to be accomplished by means of that preaching. But during the second half of the Middle Ages preaching remained in the service of the Papal hierarchy. There was then no Press, as there is now. The pulpit was the place from which public opinion made itself heard. It was in a certain measure a substitute for the press. Imagine

a time when the force that influenced public opinion
lay exclusively in the hands of the Papacy! It was a
tremendous power. We can understand that the world
of the Middle Ages must have been virtually in the
power of the Papacy. Advancing more and more from
the eleventh century onward, the supremacy not only
of the strictly ecclesiastical, but of the ascetic, the
monastic views of life increased. The State itself was
claimed as a creation of the Church. According to
ecclesiastical doctrine, first clearly enunciated by Bernard of Clairvaux, the two swords, the temporal as well
as the spiritual, belonged to the Pope (Luke xxii. 38).
Consequently the Emperor held his authority as a fief
from the Pope. The State was in itself an unholy
thing. It must first be sanctified by its connection
with the Church. And even as the star of empire faded
so the splendour of the court and of chivalry paled
before the Church and its influence. However deeply
the life of the nobles themselves was rooted in the
traditions of the Church in the twelfth and thirteenth
centuries, they had, notwithstanding, produced their
own independent view of the world, directed towards
the noble enjoyment of life and the formation of a
magnificent chivalry, a view which found enduring
expression in the laws and the aims of courtly life in all
its forms. That age, which brought forth the Crusades
and the monastic Orders of Knights, was also the
blossoming-time of this more purely worldly knighthood, with its service of chivalric love, its troubadour
poesy, its love-songs and its love of art, its brilliant
feasts and tournaments, its passion for noble combat
and adventure, its code of knightly honour and of
knightly life. The monastic ideal of renunciation was

here confronted by an ideal of noble delight in the world, which, in its extravagance in the field of love and arms, not unreasonably challenged the direct opposition of the Church. But the Mendicant Orders proved more powerful than the knights. The fact that, no later than the interregnum, the power of courtly chivalry was shattered after it had flourished for scarce a century (the classic age of chivalry begins no earlier than under Frederick Barbarossa), was owing in no small measure to the greater power of the impressive preaching of the friars, an influence which was spread abroad everywhere by the Mendicant Orders. The chivalric ideal gave way to the monastic.

## § 27. *Spiritual Law and Jurisdiction*

In the same manner temporal jurisdiction gave way to spiritual jurisdiction, and temporal law to spiritual law. In the thirteenth century the *Corpus juris canonici* (the better part of which consists of the Papal laws laid down by men like Alexander III. and Innocent III.) was placed by the side of the Roman *Corpus juris civilis*. In the Middle Ages Roman law held good as universal law. German, French, or English law could only claim the value of national law. But ecclesiastical law, in the form of the *Corpus juris canonici*, sprang up beside Roman universal law as equally valid. In the Papal code of laws the world received a second *Corpus juris*, which at the same time claimed authority to reform the ancient and imperial law of the *Corpus juris civilis* according to the requirements of that age. And upon the superiority of this ecclesiastical law, which with its prudent restrictions had entered on the inheritance of

Roman Law, depended the superiority of spiritual jurisdiction, which became even more clearly prominent after
the end of the thirteenth century.  While temporal
jurisdiction was conducted, and this more especially in
Germany, after the antiquated models of legal procedure
which had become ever more rigorously formal, lifeless,
and narrow-minded, in spiritual jurisdiction there appeared an essentially informal method of legal procedure
which looked first of all to the justice and equity of the
cause.  It was the form of legal procedure to which the
future belonged.

The power to pass judgment, to develop law, to
guide public opinion, to determine the ideal of life; the
decisive vote in all great public affairs of the West;
supremacy over emperors and knights—all this was in
the hands of the Church, and therefore of the Pope.  In
the very beginning of the thirteenth century, Pope
Innocent III. (1198-1216), who disposed of the thrones
of Germany, of England, and of Aragon, and who, as the
'Vicar of Christ and of God,' had raised the temporal
supremacy of the Papacy to its highest summit, delivered
the oracular sentence: 'The Lord has given not only the
whole Church, but the whole world, to Saint Peter to
govern.'  This sentence was the expression of the fact
which gave to the twelfth and thirteenth centuries their
peculiar character: that the palm of supreme sovereignty
belonged neither to emperors nor kings, but to the
Popes.

## § 28. *The Mendicant Orders and the Middle Class*

The Mendicant Orders were of importance in other
ways besides spreading abroad the idea of the Church
and of the Papacy.  They were significant at the same

time of the beginning of that social development which brought the Middle Class upon the stage of history.

Hitherto the history of the Middle Ages has been a history of the nobles and the clergy; and the clergy again, that is, its more influential members, came from the ranks of the nobles, from those higher grades of society distinguished by the possession of land and by knighthood. It might indeed occasionally happen that the son of an artisan was made Pope, as in the case of Gregory VII. But, as a rule, bishoprics and abbacies were occupied by members of the great families of high rank, and even among the monks, the noble and better born formed a decided majority; while in the lower ranks of the secular clergy a lower element, largely drawn from the servile classes, preponderated. Men like Ekkehard and Notker, who founded the fame of the monastery of St. Gallen, belonged to the noble families of Swabia. Bernard of Clairvaux, the pride of the Cistercians, sprang from an ancient noble family of Burgundy, and when he entered the monastery he brought more than thirty of his noble comrades with him. The whole movement begun by the monks of Cluny, which, in the eleventh, and notably the twelfth century, was a prelude to the ascetic reform of Monasticism, had its rise in the ranks of the nobles. It was their connection with the noble and landed classes of the nation which was in every case the foundation of the wealth of the monasteries, and thus also of their decay. In the Church, as in the world, the noble classes, provided as they were with landed property, were the influential leaders and representatives of the development of history. The citizen and peasant class, as far as history is concerned, as yet were not. They formed the large but uninfluential mass of the lower and, for the most part, uneducated secular clergy, which, generally speaking, stood far below the monastic clergy. It helped to prepare the economical foundations of national life ; but it represented no ideal. Civic life itself had as yet no independent intellectual character. The citizen class certainly freed itself, in the course of the twelfth and thirteenth centuries, from forced service and feudal burdens, and even from the rule, not only of the higher, but of the lower, that is, the civic or patrician nobility. But as yet the merchants and the artisans had no personal interests of their own which extended beyond the walls of the town. They lived in the interests of a narrow ecclesiastical particularism, while the whole Western world formed the horizon of the nobles and the clergy.

From the fourteenth century there dates a progressive movement of the middle class, which indeed principally began with the Mendicant Orders, and by means of their influence. The Mendicant Orders had power to demand the entry of the masses of the nation into the cloisters. In contrast to the old Orders with their aristocratic stamp, there appeared the Mendicants with their broad humanity, accessible to each and all. The time now came when the monasteries and convents began to be filled from the lower, and especially from the citizen classes. The power which was exercised by the Mendicant Orders, and above all by the Dominicans, represented at the same time the first great manifestation of the power of the middle class, and it was not in vain that the noble, courtly life of chivalry gave way before the stronger instincts—at once ascetic and civic —of the Mendicant Monks.

In the Mendicant Orders, preaching, the power of the Word, became the possession of the middle class. But not the spoken Word merely; the literature also of the thirteenth, fourteenth, and fifteenth centuries was predominantly in the hands of the Mendicant friars, and chiefly of the Dominicans again. The great intellectual movement which began in the twelfth century, at the same time as the Crusades, further gave rise to the Universities in Italy, France, England, and, after the fourteenth century, in Germany also. The majority of the professorships were occupied by Mendicant friars, especially by the Dominicans, who were distinguished by the fame of their learning. From the professorial chair, as from the pulpit, and in literature as in education, the Mendicant friar attained the first place, and the successes of learning and study, literary activity, and oratorical talent, were at the same time owing to the middle class, which in the Mendicant Orders learned for the first time to know and use the power of education.

That education, which by means of the Mendicant Orders the middle class received, and which it represented, was an ecclesiastical education, and it culminated in the foundation of the supremacy of spiritual above temporal interests, of the Papacy above the Empire. The power of the Church and of the Papacy appeared to be established on an indestructible basis. The middle class also, which advanced in a great body to claim the future for its own, was instinct with the sacerdotal and ascetic spirit; and it was now that it gave to the ideals of the Church their full weight, their unbounded supremacy over the life of the nation.

Yet in the selfsame moment the way was prepared

for the fall of the Mediæval Church, and of the whole fabric of the world it had created. The complete triumph of the Church brought with it the inevitable reaction.

### § 29. *Encroachments of the Papal Authority—Abuses*

In the course of the thirteenth century the Papacy had triumphantly overthrown the proud Hohenstaufen family. The defeat of this great rival was the visible sign of the triumph so hardly fought for. There were no more limits to the power of the Papacy, either by temporal or by spiritual law. The sum of all earthly powers was united in the Papacy as in a centre. But this very excess of power was of necessity dangerous to it.

Supremacy over the Church was practically shown in the nomination to spiritual offices. Whoever held the right of nomination had the Church also in his power. He had further at his disposal the benefices also, the immeasurable wealth of the Church, which extended over the whole world. From the twelfth century onwards the Papacy proceeded on the principle that all power of nomination in the whole Church belonged to it by law, and that therefore the Pope had the right to reserve for his own free disposal whatever places he chose, whether bishoprics, canonries, or livings. And he had, more especially, in view the right of nomination to the rich prebends of the canons. The Pope disposed of benefices in England, Germany, France, and elsewhere; at first by request to any one who properly held the right of nomination, and then by command. This was an enormous extension of the papal authority. No monarch of the world ever had at his disposal such an inexhaustible supply of benefices honours, revenues, to gain men or to reward them, as the Pope. All the possessions of the Church lay ready to his hand. But not for the advantage of the Church. Nomination within the diocese, by which the most suitable candidate was sought for the living, or the canonry, demanded that individual local and personal knowledge which was possessed by the bishop alone, who was on the spot, and not by the Pope, who was at a distance. The claim to the right of direct nomination to livings and canonries, as well as bishoprics throughout Christendom, meant the diversion of such nomination from its purpose. Not the Church and the people, but the power of the Papacy alone, was served thereby. Benefices might be, and too often were, given neither to the worthiest candidate nor to one belonging to the country, and intimate with the people and all the relations of their life, but to a stranger who had never seen either the country or the people, who probably never came to administer his office in person, whose only care was for the revenues of the living, and who let himself be represented by some hungry vicar in the duties belonging to it. Favourites of the Pope sometimes managed to secure a number of livings, perhaps in various countries, where any serious administration of the office was out of the question. On the other hand, it sometimes happened that the same livings would be given to several candidates, to one directly, and to another by expectance, as it was called, on the death of the first. Nay, more, reversions of the same living were frequently given to different candidates, so that when the living became vacant, it might be doubtful to whom it belonged, and the most troublesome law-suits would arise. But one thing was always clear, that what the candidate had in his mind was the revenue, not the office. The Church fell into the hands of hirelings. The people and local authorities were not always satisfied with the appointment of an interloper assigned to them from a distance and nominated by the Pope. It became necessary for the Pope's nominee to be accompanied, in addition to the Papal despatch, by Papal agents empowered to instal him forcibly. He appeared on the scene under somewhat trying circumstances. In the year 1350 the King of England, together with his parliament, passed a resolution to suffer no more Papal agents on English territory. The Papal right of nomination was regarded as little better than a robbery of the country in favour of the political power of the Papacy, and, still worse, of strangers, Italians and Frenchmen, who formed the Pope's immediate surroundings ; and it was therefore decided that England and English benefices were to be kept for Englishmen. Already the national interest was arrayed against the mediæval idea of a universal Papacy.

And not the interest of the nation alone, but the nearest interests of bishops and parish priests were attacked by the wide encroachments of the Papal authority. Even by the Pope's interference with the nominations, the position of a bishop in his diocese must have been seriously shaken. But now came a more important matter—the appearance of the Mendicant Orders and their power. Through their numerous privileges they were protected from all exertions of episcopal and parochial authority as by a 'wide sea.' The bishop had nothing to do with them ; the Mendicants were directly subject to the Pope. The parish priest could not deny them his pulpit and his congregation. The Mendicant friar came and ministered to the spiritual needs of the congregation ; he came and preached ; he came and heard confession ; he even came and passed sentence of excommunication. By means of the privileges he held from the Pope, he had a right to absolve and to chastise more extensive than that of the parish priest, or even the bishop himself. No wonder if the Mendicant monk was preferred to the priest in the confessional, and especially in the cure of souls. The priest could not prevent the Mendicant monk from becoming the minister and pastor of his people rather than himself. The regular constitution of the Church sank before the Papal privileges. The weight of the Papal authority crushed to the earth the fabric of ecclesiastical organization which rested on bishops and on priests.

All that yet remained of episcopal authority was destroyed by appeals to the Pope. Ever since the time of Gregory VII., appeals to Rome had been systematically favoured by the Popes ; not only when it was merely a question of judgment to be pronounced, but in all cases of ecclesiastical administration. Soon there was no single act of ecclesiastical administration which could not be referred to the Pope by way of appeal. Not only the entire system of nomination, but the entire administration of the Church, was in the last resort united in the Papacy ; the whole Church was to receive its government directly from Rome. But it was obviously impossible to bring for final decision all particular questions of local administration, with every doubtful case of nomination, or of disciplinary or other rule, to a single place, the Papal Court. The decision made there must have often miscarried, must have been often determined by the merest accident, or, what was worse, by bribery or other personal influence. And the long journey to the Papal court, the residence in the distant city, the encounter with all the inconveniences of a foreign land, must have involved considerable hardship for the bishops and clergy. Among the cases of nomination which were 'reserved' for the Pope, were those benefices which became vacant by the death of the holder of the benefice during his residence at the Papal court. The fact spoke volumes for the administration of justice. Along with the swarm of place-hunters at the Papal court, there thronged the whole crowd of those who had expectations from the decision of some point of law or of administration ; and often enough the expectant candidate was struck down by death before the decision could be made.

The excess of the Papal rights, not only of nomination but of administration, as well as the excess of the privileges showered by the Pope chiefly on the Mendicant Orders, must be regarded as a hindrance to the healthy development of the Church. The Papacy hitherto had been the guiding and organizing power in the Church, but now that its power was turned into omnipotence, it became a factor of dissolution and disorganization.

And so much the more so when, in the service of Papal authority, not only temporal, but purely financial ends were made more and more prominent. With a bold idealism, Gregory VII. had founded the supremacy of the Papacy as a purely spiritual authority. But his

successors in the fourteenth century laid themselves
out to use the authority of the 'Vicar of God upon
earth,' as a means to the lowest pursuit of gain.   The
revenues which flowed into the Papal court from all
parts of Christendom were enormous.   The annates, the
dues for the 'pallium,' and the taxes paid for dispensation, were found especially burdensome.   Annates
were a duty, generally amounting to half of the year's
income, which had to be paid in advance by every one
who held a benefice from the Papal court.   Dues for
the 'pallium' consisted of the very considerable sums
which every archbishop had to pay in return for the
*pallium* (a cape of white woollen material), which he
received from the Pope.   When a benefice changed
hands often, it soon became over-burdened with debt ;
the dues had generally to be borne by the whole
province, because the archbishop was seldom able to
raise them out of his own means.   As for taxes on
dispensations, the Pope himself had made the laws from
the observance of which he granted dispensation, so
that he was loudly blamed for making laws with a view
to the taxes raised thereby.

But the worst offence was that simony (that is, the
sale of spiritual offices or ecclesiastical benefices for
money) was openly practised at the Papal court.   This
meant that there they alone could succeed with their
lawsuit, their petition, or their election, who had money
to spend with a free hand.   The whole retinue of the
Pope, from the porter to the cardinal, exacted their
proportion of tribute from the petitioner.   It was a
shameful spectacle of abuse.   Corruption reigned in the
place to which all Christendom looked for the stimulus
to its moral and religious life.

## § 30. *The Babylonian Exile—Schism*

The severe fall which the Papacy experienced early in the fourteenth century was a symptom of its inner dissolution. The fourteenth century was the period of what is known as the 'Babylonian exile' in Avignon. After the fall of the imperial house of Hohenstaufen, France, which was already striving to become a united State, while Germany was broken up into a number of territorial sovereignties, appeared as a great power. Boniface VIII. (1294-1303), who had made the claims of Papal supremacy felt in all their strength, was involved in a severe conflict with Philip the Fair of France on this point. Boniface directed against Philip his famous Bull '*Unam sanctam*' (1302), which claimed for the Church, with unhesitating and determined force, the power not only to wield the temporal sword, but to create and to depose kings. But here the Papacy met finally with an overthrow. Pope Clement V. (1305-1314) was compelled by Philip the Fair to declare formally (1306) that France and the power of the French king were not touched by the Bull '*Unam sanctam.*' Philip the Fair even succeeded further, in compelling Clement to remove the seat of the Papacy from Rome to Avignon (1309). Avignon was the property of the Pope, but it lay in the immediate neighbourhood of the French royal territory. What the proud race of Hohenstaufen had not succeeded in accomplishing was now attained in a few years by the French kings, a race newly risen, but one which anticipated the idea of modern statesmanship. At the same time that the Papacy proclaimed as a principle that the range of its authority was unlimited, and, as an instance

thereof, claimed authority in the person of Pope
John XXII. (1316-1334) over kingdom and emperor, in
opposition to Louis of Bavaria, it was then practically
the vassal of the French king and a tool in his hands.
It was the undue extension of its claims to supremacy
which led the Papacy into conflict with the authority
of the State, which was gradually growing conscious of
power, and thus brought about its overthrow.    The
Babylonian exile in Avignon lasted from the year 1305
till 1377, from the time of Clement V. to that of
Gregory XI.—that is, during nearly the whole of the
fourteenth century.    In all the Church it was felt to be
a disenthroning and captivity of the Papacy, and, in a
certain measure, of the Church itself.    Hence the continual attempts to do away with the innovation.    After
1378 there arose a Pope in Rome in opposition to the
Pope in Avignon.    Christendom was divided into two
hostile camps.    The Papacy, so long the pillar of unity
within the Church, was now become the cause of a
schism.    The two supreme heads of Christendom fought
each other with ban and interdict.    The nations of the
West saw for the first time that even the thunderbolt
of Papal excommunication could fall harmless to the
earth.    As long as the Papacy was at war with itself,
it effaced with its own weapons the impression of its
authority.    The division lasted more than thirty years,
—from 1378 to 1409.    In the year 1409 a council was
summoned at Pisa, which was to heal the schism.    It
deposed the two rival Popes and appointed a third, but
it had no power to carry its decision into execution.
The two rival Popes remained ; the Pope elected at Pisa
was merely a third rival.    The two-headed schism
had become a three-headed one (1409-1417).    Papal

supremacy came to an end in the beginning of the
fifteenth century with a fearful overthrow. Ruin
without and ruin within was the bitter fruit of that
supremacy so hardly won.

## § 31. *Degradation of Monasticism*

Not only the Papacy, but Monasticism, had by its
very successes prepared the way for its decline. The
thirteenth, and notably the fourteenth, century was, as
we have seen, the period when the monasteries and
convents had decidedly gained the upper hand by
means of the relations they had established with the
middle class. But that very movement of the masses
which filled the cloisters of the Mendicants, was of
necessity fatal to them. There were too many who
took their oaths without the necessary inward calling.
Too many entered the cloisters to escape, not the world
and its sins, but the necessity of work. Many a cloister
became more like a society of idlers than a society of
ascetics, and called more for censure than for reverence.
At the spectacle of this mode of existence, steadily
increasing and supported by beggary as it was, the
question involuntarily arose among the class of citizens
and peasants, whether it is really more pleasing to God
to do nothing, and to live by the labour of others, than
to fulfil our duties honestly in some worldly calling.
It had now become unmistakably clear that the principle
of Monasticism was incapable of practical application
to the whole of Christendom. And could that principle
be really regarded as the ideal of a Christian's life
which could only be realized on the condition that the
majority of mankind remained in a worldly calling and

put up with a lower form of Christianity? Yet more. It soon became evident that the sharpening of asceticism introduced by the Mendicants was powerless to support the rigorous and truly monastic spirit. Immorality and licentiousness spread even among the Mendicants themselves. The fourteenth and fifteenth centuries echo to the cry raised against the immorality of monks, nuns, and clergy. It would be unjust to overlook the fact that the better element—the more perfectly educated, spiritually and morally—was largely represented even at this period. But the average of the great mass of the monks and clergy were sunk below the normal standard of morality. While the Mendicants had laid themselves out to conquer the world of that time, it became manifest that the most rigorous ascetic law was powerless to overcome the sinful impulses of human nature. They went the way of all Orders: upon a period of ascendency there followed a period of decline, a decline the more fatal in proportion to the greatness of the claims made at the outset, above all, to the greatness of the movement of the masses who took part in their ruin as in their rise.

## § 32. *Reforming Forces*

The Mediæval Church with its greatest products, the Papacy and Monasticism, had reached the term of its natural development. The Papacy was sinking under the weight of its own mighty claims, and had become a source of countless abuses, and even a cause of schism. Monasticism had unduly extended the claims of asceticism, and had ended in moral bankruptcy. The Church and the world longed after a new spring of life. The time had come for the reformation of the Church in head and members.

There were none who did not share in this longing. The consciousness of the need for reformation was deep and universal. Nay, more, the powers had already appeared which bore the splendour of the coming day. The fourteenth and fifteenth centuries were not wholly an age of decline. They were the age which nursed the Reformation. The great work which was to be completed was preceded by an intellectual movement which was to lead to his goal the chosen champion of God.

Already the English Wiclif (died 1384), under the pressure of the great schism and of the utter corruption of the Papacy and the clergy, had declared the Pope to be Antichrist, rejected the Church's claims to power over the State, proclaimed war against the Mendicant friars, enthroned the Bible as the only pure source of God's Word, and the only rule of ecclesiastical doctrine. Already John Huss, his zeal kindled by the writings of Wiclif, had attacked the principle of the infallibility of Papal decrees and the power of indulgences. As with the mighty Wiclif, so was it with Huss, Wiclif's true follower till death. His nation stood by him, and at the fire of the stake, at which, by the judgment of the Council of Constance, Huss perished as a heretic (1415), was kindled the great insurrection of Bohemia, not only against its king, Sigismund, who had given his consent to the martyrdom of Huss, but against the Roman Church; an insurrection which was only ended in the year 1433, by the treaty of peace concluded between the Council of Basel and the Hussites, which granted the administration of the cup to the laity.

Already in Germany, by means of the mysticism of men like Master Eckart (Strasburg, 1312-17 ; died at Cologne in 1328) and Tauler (died at Strasburg, 1361), there was spread abroad a spirit of piety which turned with longing from the outward forms of the Church to an inner communion with God. The 'Friends of God,' who arose after the middle of the fourteenth century in Upper Germany and Switzerland, and the 'Brothers of the Common Life,' who appeared after the end of the same century in Holland and Germany, had generated among the widespread ranks of the laity a form of Christianity which was a return to the Bible, and an earnest search for salvation, and which manifested itself in active self-denying love. Thomas à Kempis, the famous author of the *Imitation of Christ*, and Johann Wessel, the forerunner of Luther in biblical theology, arose from the ranks of the 'Brothers of the Common Life.'

In the same period of the fourteenth and fifteenth centuries which witnessed the decline of the Papacy and the clergy, and the overthrow of the spiritual and moral forces of mediæval ecclesiasticism, there arose more and more a passionate longing, which was felt more in Germany than in any other land, for a true Christianity, united and reformed. It was at this very period that Germany became adorned with those magnificent churches which form to this day the ornament of her towns, and with those countless pious institutions also, which witness unmistakably to the spiritual life of the German citizens. At this very period, more especially as we approach the end of the fifteenth century, there appeared a religious literature which aimed at the widest possible circulation, a hortatory

literature which spoke in the language of the people ;
nay, more, there appeared a translation of the Bible
itself. As the citizen class increased, it longed for
inward possession of Christianity. Hence its sympathy
with the Mendicants (see § 28), and, at the same time,
its insistence on a popular treatment of spiritual things
which could reach the multitude and come home to all
ranks of the population. The same great endeavour
after the ideal, which in the Germany of the fourteenth
and fifteenth centuries caused one University after
another to grow up, as it were, with the exuberance of
spring-tide, found its expression, not only in its churches
and institutions, and in the peculiar style and the
strength of its religious literature, but in the desire for
the highest things, a desire as yet not fully conscious
but which was universally felt. At the same period,
there appeared on the horizon the art and learning of
the ancient world, which was born again in the Italian
renaissance, and with gigantic force tore asunder the
fetters of mediæval tradition. The world felt the overthrow of the mediæval spirit. Therefore did it hunger
after a new spirit, and in this strong and universal
yearning after the intellectual and spiritual there lay the
upward tendency which prepared the way for things to
come. The Reformation itself was preceded by a longing
after a reformation, as a sign that the time was come.

The West rose up like one man to the work of
reformation, under the leadership, first of its spiritual,
then of its temporal princes.

### § 33. *The Councils of Reform*

The bishops were the first to approach the great
problem. The Council of Pisa (1409), which was re-

ferred to above, was the first, if a useless attempt, of this kind. By this time no less than three popes stood in opposition to each other. It was a scandal to Christendom. On the strength of this feeling rested the power of the movement which was produced by the great Council of Constance (1414-1418). Bishops from all parts of Western Christendom were assembled there, together with numerous representatives of the universities and of theological science. The Emperor Sigismund himself took part in the Council. The power of the assembly answered to its splendour, a power which rested on the unanimous desire of the West for the reformation of the Church by means of the Council. First of all the Council had to assume the authority necessary for its work. As it was a question of the reformation of the Papacy, of the head itself, and more particularly of the healing of the schism, the assembly had to claim for itself authority over the Papacy. So it came to pass. The assembly determined that the supreme authority in the Church should belong not to the Pope but to a General Council—that the general assembly of bishops stands above the Pope. In exercise of this supreme authority the three rival popes were forthwith deposed by a resolution of the Council : that is, they were compelled to resign, and a new Pope, Martin V., was installed (1417). The powerful position of the Council was shown by the fact that the new Pope was generally recognized, and the schism actually healed. At the same time, the bishops as a united body were placed above the Papacy, so that a regressive movement was begun which was to do away with the ecclesiastical monarchy of Gregory VII. and bring back the old aristocratic constitution of the

Church. But with this effort the power of the Council
was exhausted. The continuation of the work of reformation was reserved for a new General Council which
was to be convoked. The Council of Basel (1431-1443),
convoked by Pope Martin a short while before his
death, was the heir and the continuation of the Council
of Constance. But the opposition of Pope Eugenius IV.,
and of the party favourable to the Papacy, was a
hindrance to every thorough-going regulation. Annates
were done away with, limits were put to the appeals to
Rome, resolutions were passed against Papal reservations and against the possession of concubines by the
clergy. That was all. When the council would have
proceeded further, it was dispersed by the order of the
Pope for its removal to Ferrara (1437). What was left
at Basel was a 'Rump' of a Council, which, after a
useless struggle with the Pope, came to an inglorious
end in the year 1443. The power of the councils was
destroyed ; the work of reformation undertaken by the
bishops had failed. It did not last long ; and Pope
Pius II. (1458-1464), who, at the Council of Basel, had
been himself a champion of the reform party, was able
to punish every appeal to a General Council with excommunication as heresy (1459). The Papacy once
more seized on the reins of ecclesiastical authority.
The claim of the Episcopate to power by means of
their councils became a mere episode.

## § 34. *Power of the Sovereigns*

Nevertheless, the old unlimited authority of the Pope
never came to life again. By this time the authority
of the State had arisen, and became every day more

conscious of its power. The mediæval idea of universal
supremacy, upon which the authority of popes and
emperors had rested, gave place to the growing feeling
of nationality, and, together with the modern national
consciousness, there was awakened a national political
authority which gained an ever clearer comprehension
of the problems before it. In France and England
the royal power arose, a living power, deeply rooted in
the life of the people. In Spain, after a long conflict,
the last remnant of Moorish supremacy was destroyed,
and Ferdinand the Catholic reigned supreme over the
whole Peninsula. The age of the great monarchies
was at hand. In Germany the movement was less
favourable to the Empire than to the territorial States
under the sway of their own sovereigns; but it was in
these States that a way was prepared for the German
State of the future. The suppression of the councils
was principally owing to the Pope's possession of the
right of ecclesiastical government, and especially the
right of nomination, by which he held the temporal
princes in his own hands. Under Ferdinand the
Catholic, the government of the Spanish Church was
transferred to the Crown. The same thing happened,
in the beginning of the sixteenth century, in England
under Henry VIII., where the government of the Papal
legate, Cardinal Wolsey, who was furnished with full
authority by the Pope, meant in point of fact the
government of the Church by the king of England. In
the year 1517 the power of nomination to the French
bishoprics was placed in the hands of the king of
France. The German sovereigns received similar rights.
The age of ecclesiastical government had passed away,
and the age was preparing in which Luther could

summon the Christian nobles of the German nation
to the work of reformation. The temporal princes
obtained possession of the Church and sought to bring
about reform on their own account by their own method
of nomination and by political superintendence of
ecclesiastical life.

But had the State power to pour new life into the
Church? Did the Church of England become another
because it was now ruled by a king instead of a pope?
With the advancing power of the State the Western
Church was shattered. There arose the Spanish, the
French or Gallic, and the English national churches,
and when the Pope refused to Henry VIII. the divorce
for which he had applied, there needed but the word of
a king to separate the Church of England from the
body of the Church, and this at first without any kind
of inner reform. The government of the State resulted
in the dissolution, but not in the improvement of the
Church.

The entire work of the bishops in their councils, and
of the State by means of its right of ecclesiastical
government, was merely a change in the Church's
constitution. Another fashion was given to the outer
garment of the Church. But that which was required was not a change of constitution, but a change
of spirit, an upspringing of new forces from the depths
of the religious life and of the Church's being, from the
inexhaustible well of the Gospel which the Church still
bears for ever within her—a work which neither princes
nor kings, neither bishops nor popes could accomplish,
but God alone. The angel of God had to come down
to trouble the waters of the Church, and give them new
healing power.

# DIVISION III

# THE AGE OF THE REFORMATION

## CHAPTER I

### REFORMATION

### § 35. *New Currents*

IF we make our way into Germany about the year 1500, we read over the arch of the door through which we enter, inscribed in golden letters, the word : Renaissance. A cry of joy rings through the whole cultivated world. Rejoice ! Rejoice ! The world of classical antiquity is transfigured, is born again in all the loveliness of youth. Here is the true Aristotle ; here is the divine Plato ; here are the master-works of art and learning, full of marvellous beauty and immortal intellect—and the sun of Homer shines even upon us.

It was the age of Raphael and Michael Angelo. It was the age when an aspiring race, full of passionate ambition and enthusiasm, thirsting for life, and longing after all that was great, was fired by the sublime power of ancient literature and learning ; when the universalism of the Middle Ages was displaced by a national spirit, fashioned after the heroic forms and nourished on the political ideals of the ancient world ; when the middle class gained strength and came into the foreground of history ;

when it found and welcomed in the new learning a power all its own, an educating power which freed it from the guardianship of the Church, which committed the cultivation of learning chiefly to the hands of the citizen class, and made the towns the permanent centres of intellectual life. Life itself took another form. The spirit of the ancient world rose up against monastic asceticism ; it spread around it a new joy in life and beauty, a sense for all that makes life graceful, an enthusiasm for the nation and the state. On the whole world it shed a rosy light.

The sound of a new Gospel of Culture went forth from Italy and filled the West. Mediæval ideas and theories gave way before the spirit of the ancient world in its resurrection. A new age approached, a mother age that bore in its fruitful bosom a future full of inexhaustible promise.

Yet was this the new birth which the fifteenth century longed for so ardently? Was this the Gospel which the ageing world of the Middle Ages desired the spring

'Wherefrom to drink new youth, new life again'?

By no means. That which the world of the Middle Ages desired in its innermost heart was not Renaissance, but Reformation ; not the regeneration of art and learning, but the regeneration of the Church in its head and all its members ; not the glad tidings of the re-discovery of the ancient world, but the glad tidings which are preached to the poor, which can bring blessedness to sinners, and regenerate all mankind. Moral renaissance, through the renewal of the Church's life—this was the greatest and highest aim

for which the forces of the fifteenth century were
stirred again and again in one united movement.  In
the abuses of the Church, in the degradation of spiritual
things, in the troubling and stopping of those springs
from which the commonwealth draws its moral nourish-
ment, the instinct of the age recognised with unerring
certainty the cause of the widespread corruption.  The
Church was merged in the world.  The salt had lost its
savour.  The claims of Christianity were trodden under
foot, mostly of those who were called to be vessels of
faith, preachers of divine truth and examples to their
flock.  The decay of the Church was a crying evil,
felt most strongly wherever the longing after spiritual
things was most widespread, as it was in Germany.
Therefore, through all the joy of the Renaissance,
through all the rejoicing which breaks forth from the
renewing of the life of art and learning, ever and ever
louder the great cry resounds all through the fifteenth
century : 'Reformation of the Church in head and
members !'  Reformation, not merely of the scholarly
and æsthetic life, but of that which is far harder—the
religious life.

We have seen the great Councils of Reform at
Constance and Basel whose proceedings fill the whole
of the first half of the fifteenth century.  The desire for
the Church's reformation was as a great flood bearing
all the West before it, and its aim was almost to sweep
away the Papacy itself with all its abuses.  Those were
magnificent plans and hopes ; yet they all miscarried.
We have seen the great political powers which in the
second half of the century took in hand the work of
reformation.  By means of the political rights of nomination and superintendence, new power was to be given

back to the clergy, and to the Church the spirit of
a Church.  But it was all a hopeless labour at the
mere outworks of the Church; instead of an inward
regeneration, it was a dissolution of the Western
Church into a number of national churches striving
for independence.

But, it may be said, could not the culture of the
age, the bold and powerful progress of the Renaissance,
bring about the desired improvement of the Church?
Unfortunately, this culture was pagan to the very core.
It had no thought of reformation, rather it was prepared
to submit outwardly and with no great struggle to the
power of the Church, with all its ceremonies and all its
claims; for in its inmost heart it was indifferent to all
that was Christian; it had no care but for what was
purely human.  The Renaissance of art and learning
was no new birth of morality.  It was the Renaissance
rather which, while it re-awakened the heroic ideal of
the ancient world, yet filled the cities and states of Italy
with violent, remorseless, haughty tyrants, who thirsted
for power and glory, and whose geniality was only
attained by contempt for all laws of morality.  Never
was there a society so brilliant in its culture, so full of
interests and rich in natural talents, so full of the
creative power which revealed itself in immortal master-
pieces, and yet which was at its heart so immoral, so
corrupt, so full of selfish animalism, as Italian Society
in the second half of the fifteenth century.  This was
the age which produced a Cæsar Borgia, at once its
image, its ideal, and its terror.  This was the age in
which Machiavelli wrote his *Prince*, which was both
a manual for princes and a glorification of their coldest,
most remorseless, calculating and cruel selfishness.  Even

when we look upon all those pictures of Madonnas and
of saints, and, first of all, upon Raphael's wonderful
creations, the predominating impression is that of mere
humanity, however beautiful, glorious, and transfigured.
Seldom do the mysteries of Christianity shine upon us
with overpowering beauty, as from the eyes of the Sistine
Madonna.

As for the Papacy of the Renaissance, in the persons
of men like Innocent VIII. (1484-1492) and Alexander
VI.[1] (1492-1503), the deep-seated immorality of that
age, stained as it was with murder, treachery, and
licentiousness, ascended the papal throne.  They were
followed by Julius II. (1503-1513), a general rather
than a pope, the work of whose life was war and outrage,
with the view of aggrandizing the ecclesiastical state
and giving to it internal political unity.  Julius was
succeeded by Leo X. (1513-1521), the fine connoisseur,
the man of high culture, the patron of Raphael and
Michael Angelo.

What were the impulses which gave to the Church
leaders like these?  The Papacy of Leo X. is great in
the history of culture, insignificant in the history of the
Church.  The Renaissance which produced these popes
also caused them to set their hearts upon earth and
worldly things, and brought it to pass that the pope
who, with a light heart, sold to temporal princes the
interests of the united Church, with all rights of nomination and of government, made the establishment of an
ecclesiastical state his foremost interest, and was transformed from the supreme head of the universal spiritual
monarchy to one of those Italian tyrants who were

---

[1] His son, as is well known, was Cæsar Borgia, his daughter, Lucretia
Borgia.

either voluptuous and cruel, or violent and warlike, or
else wholly interested in art and learning. The interests
of the Renaissance were fundamentally opposed to the
interests of the Church; so that the high tide of intellectual life, which about the year 1500 swept the
Western world along with it, brought no deliverance
but seemed rather to hasten the final ruin.

In Germany, certainly, the intellectual development
took a somewhat different direction. It was pre-eminently the scene of that great movement of reform which
in the fifteenth century shook the whole world through
the Councils of Constance and of Basel. Here, even
now in the beginning of the sixteenth century, spiritual
interests were still in strong preponderance. These
were the interests in which all classes of the nation
could feel that they had a share. It was they which
gave to the German Renaissance, to Humanism itself, a
decidedly spiritual tendency. Those great desires which
can only find satisfaction in Christianity had their life
too deep in the heart of the nation; the strength with
which the people longed after the certainty of its soul's
salvation was too powerful for it to forget in anything
else the object of its supreme longing. So it came
to pass that Humanism gave the Bible afresh, in its
original languages, into the hands of the educated classes
(the New Testament through Erasmus of Rotterdam,
the Old Testament through Reuchlin); and that the
value of philology was recognized in order that theology
also might be helped to a better knowledge of its
original sources. Nay, more, it was hoped that a study
of the Scriptures in the light of philology would be the
direct means of bringing the Church to life again. But
this learned movement, which in Germany pointed as

with an uplifted finger to the New Testament, was far from being able to make any marked impression on the masses of the people, or to put an end to the corruption of the Church. To begin with, it laid hold on the educated classes alone, and influenced these only through the impulse it gave to investigation, and not through the living steadfast power of accomplished results. Certainly the German humanists were not indifferent to the Church in the same way as were their fellow-students in Italy. But their culture wanted the fiery force given by great positive convictions. So it came about that the great intellect and knowledge with which these men were gifted, as far as the Church was concerned, exploded in the fire-works of ridicule and satire (see for instance Erasmus' *Praise of Folly*, 1509) which they showered on the abuses of the Church. It was a movement which, like every purely literary move-ment, was strong in denial, but weak in affirmation ; it saw well the need for which it had to fight, but it was destitute of that elementary natural force which can alone bring forth the grand creative deeds of history.

At the conclusion of the great Lateran Council in 1517 which for its part was also concerned with the reforma-tion of the Church, but was content with defining the omnipotence of the Pope and the immortality of the human soul (a work which had already become necessary in the face of the Italian ' Illumination '), the bishop of Isernia, in the closing speech which he was appointed to deliver, spoke these words : ' The Gospel is the source of all wisdom, of all virtue, of all that is divine and wonderful ; the Gospel, I say, the Gospel.' He was right, and more right than he himself knew.

Even now there had arisen that young hero who was

sent from God to proclaim everywhere the long-forgotten, the true and perfect Gospel.

## § 36. *Luther*

Help came from a quarter whence it would never
have been looked for—from the monastic order. The
monks had created the Church of the Middle Ages by
means of the movement which began in Cluny; and
through a monk that Church was to be destroyed.

The monks had become the most contemptible class
in the whole Church. They had meant to flee from the
world, they had left all behind them; but the world
that they bore in their own hearts, sinful desire and
self-seeking, unseen, but ever present, had gone forth
with them into the solitude of the wilderness and the
cloister. Even out of the heart of the monk proceeded
evil thoughts, carnal and worldly lusts. Monasticism
was swallowed up by the world which it would have
fled from; and Monasticism had become the vulnerable
point against which the humanists aimed all the arrows
of their ridicule, if they meant to scourge the iniquities
of the Church. Nevertheless, in Monasticism there still
lived, though troubled, shaken, often scarcely perceptible, the influence of the true Christian character,
which, with fear and trembling, strives after a righteousness worthy in the sight of God. And these impulses
of the religious life were to prove themselves stronger,
both to deliver and to reform the world, than all the
culture and all the great discoveries of the age. Monasticism, in its search for salvation by the renunciation of
the world, and by the works of asceticism, pressed home
upon the earnest seeker the necessity of the final conclusion: that in spite of all of them, in the sight of God,

by the works of the law shall no flesh be justified ; that all human efforts are unavailing to turn away the wrath of the just and holy God, who hates sin and visits it upon the sinner unto the fourth generation ; that even Monasticism, with all its self-torture and renunciation of the world, is in vain—it cannot earn salvation. The development of Monasticism was a sharpening of the ascetic principle that logically led to self-annihilation. This was the process of development which Luther had lived through, with all the energy of a fiery nature that was made for great things. He had felt the whole weight of the divine law in his inmost conscience. He had lived through hours in which his faith in God became an anguish, torturing soul and body, hours in which God crushed 'like a lion' the bones, as it were, of the monk who wrestled with him for his soul's salvation. Those were the hours in which God prepared the monk to be his mighty instrument. Great were the anguish and the struggles—great also was the victory. 'The just shall live by faith,' that was the melody, which, sounding ever clearer, filled his soul with heavenly ecstasy. Man shall be justified, neither by his works, nor by his self-torture, nor by his renunciation of the world, but by faith alone, through grace, through free, all-merciful, inexhaustible grace. The grace and truth revealed in Jesus Christ now shone clearly upon him, bringing peace, and lighting up the path of a life which became ever more stormy. In spite of all the inward conflicts which even later were not spared him, the newly-discovered Gospel, so long painfully withheld from him and lost so long, became 'a wide-opened door into Paradise.' He had hungered and thirsted after righteousness, and now he was filled. He had long striven after the kingdom of God, and now all had fallen to him—the blessedness of the children of God, which turns every new day into a holy day—the freedom of a Christian man, who through his faith is 'a lord over all things.'

And that which had become a blessed certainty to himself he was constrained to proclaim abroad with the voice of a trumpet over all lands. It was his enemies who urged him onwards in his great career, further and further ; until suddenly he saw the whole organization of the Church to which his inmost soul had clung so steadfastly, with all its traditions and sanctities, its priesthood and its powers, standing between him and the pure Gospel. His great work was this, that in that moment he did not hesitate for an instant to fling away from him, to give up for Christ's sake and the Gospel's, all that had hitherto seemed to him great, and glorious, and sacred, that could be neither dispensed with nor replaced. For the sake of the Gospel he became poor in all by which he had hitherto been made rich. The whole world, in and by which he had hitherto lived, fell in ruins around him. He had to give up his faith in the Church which he had so warmly loved ; but only to exchange it for a fuller and richer faith in salvation and justification through Jesus Christ. He was to lose the world of his youth, but the world of the future was to be given to him as a recompense. With one bold cast of the sling he hurled in the face of the monks with their asceticism, of the Church with its powerful hierarchy, his Gospel of justification by faith alone. It was an inexhaustible Gospel, full of reforming power, and able, not only to destroy the old, but to lead on in triumph the new age

—an age great with life, which burst asunder by its
own inward growth the fetters that bound it from
without.

Monasticism came to an end, in the person of Martin
Luther, by flinging off asceticism, together with the
monkish habit and the cloistral life, by giving up
fasting and alms - begging, by turning again to the
world, that it might no longer forsake the world, but
hallow it.

The new-born Gospel meant the reformation of the
Church ; and the reformation of the Church meant the
reformation of the whole world.

To the Middle Ages the world was a world of sin.
Therefore the piety of the Middle Ages consisted in the
renunciation of the world with all it had to give. In
this belief the monk forsook marriage, possessions, the
whole world with its art, its learning, its joys, its duties,
in order to crucify his flesh and all its lusts. It was a
magnificent sacrifice of the world and of self ; yet, alas,
in forsaking the world of sin, he forsook the world of
morality. He fled temptation, but he fled at the same
time those duties which God has laid upon the individual,
upon every individual in His world ; the duties of family
and of social life with all their demands for self-
renunciation and self-sacrifice, for a genuine, right, and
vigorous morality. The monk in his selfishness withdrew into his cell in order to live no longer to his
neighbour, but to himself alone. The door swung
behind him, and the key turned in the lock ; he saw no
longer the world with its duties ; he saw nothing but
himself. He had escaped the storms of life ; from the
sea of care and labour, from the countless calls of daily
life, he had entered into the haven of peace, leaving

others without : let them help themselves as best they might. He had escaped the battle of life ; but, alas! his flight was a cowardly forsaking of his banner.

The face of the whole world was changed by the reformation with its doctrine of justification by faith alone. Believe in the Lord Jesus Christ, so shalt thou be saved, thyself and thy whole house : that is the complete, the whole divine Gospel, that can neither be added to nor taken away from. Take its precious meaning home and be quickened thereby. Thou hast nothing to add to it. Away with self-manufactured morality and piety, the holiness of a life of ascetic renunciation. The monks will not trust in the grace of God freely offered through Christ, but would add to the grace of God a justification earned by their own efforts. God has set man in the world, not that he may forsake the world, but that he may serve God in the world. True Christian morality is to go forth into the world, to take part in all the joys and sorrows of a worldly calling, of family life, of life lived with and for our neighbours ; in order through faith in God to find the true joy which is a fresh power of victory, to find inward rest in all unrest, and, here, in the world, to see the divine, the eternal, which leads onwards to the world above. The fulfilment of duty is the true service of God. Thus faith leads us into the midst of the world, to the service of our neighbour. Thus faith brings forth the power of love, which seeks, not its own, but another's good. As faith makes the Christian lord over all things and subject of no man, so through love it makes him a ministering servant, subject to all and every man. True Christian perfection is to remain a true Christian in the midmost stress of human life, and, in the labour of the day, to fight the good fight to which the promise of victory is given.

The stain of unholiness was taken away from the world, and from life in the world. Life in a worldly calling, in the State, the society, and the family, appeared no longer as an unavoidable evil, permitted only on account of the weaker brethren, or as the glistening exterior which covers some deadly thing ; but as the natural activity of true and perfect Christian morality. All these relations of man to man bore within them duties appointed by God ; they possessed a moral worth of their own, and a power of true deliverance from the temptations of selfishness, a power which the sins of men might indeed be able to degrade, but not to extinguish altogether. Look, for instance, at marriage. It now appears as the truly holy and spiritual state. It is an order instituted by God Himself ; a means of education for the mature man, which not only gives to him wife and children, not only provides for him a refuge from the hideous ills of life, an ever new source of joy, a protecting atmosphere of living love ; but it is to him a moral discipline, through the daily duties of domestic life ; it nourishes, strengthens, and corrects ; it changes mere existence into life lived for others ; from the bosom of the home it brings to light daily those ideals which are a lesson to the educator and the teacher himself, as well as to those whom he has to educate. Look at the State. It appears no longer as a work of the devil, a work of sin or of injustice.  The State, like the family, is a divine institution, with independent moral duties of its own, appointed to make possible and to secure for man that legal freedom which is the first step to moral freedom. Look at the whole round of political life, at labour in agriculture and commerce, in handicraft and trade, in science and art, in obedience and command ; the labour of man-servant and maid, of the judge, the soldier, the official, and the prince ; look where you will, all this labour, performed as a calling ordered by God, is the service of God which is well pleasing to Him. The whole world has become holy, and all that was profane in it is done away with. The world with all its duties is changed into the vineyard of the Lord, into a temple of God, in which we are to worship Him in spirit and in truth.

With the tumult of a storm these ideas of reformation swept over the West, and particularly the German world. They have laid the foundations of the present ; nay, more, they have brought forth the moral ideals of the life of the present age. Against the mediæval ascetic ideal of renunciation, there appeared a new ideal of life, which was akin to the Renaissance, in so far as it inclined to the world, recognized and comprehended it, but which was to fill the world not with the ideals of Humanism, but with the ideals of Christianity.

Many were the moral forces set free by this revolution of thought, and brought to bear upon the life of the family, the State, and the community at large. Now, for the first time, is seen the full value of the State, of a civic calling, and of civic freedom. The modern State arises ; the moral ideals which the secular world bears within it appear in all their power, beside the moral endeavours of the Church. The secular world has become free ; it is delivered from the ban which the Church of the Middle Ages laid upon it. The secular world is reformed.

The reformation of the world was a consequence of the reformation of the Church.

The fifteenth century had attempted the same thing by making experiments with the Church's constitution, by issuing fresh rules of discipline. It was labour in vain to attempt to reform the Church by these means. When Luther attacked the doctrine of the Church and the Gospel which she preached, when he transformed and filled it with a new spirit, he touched, without at first knowing it, the single point from which the whole being and life of the Church could be set in motion and transformed. The heart of the Church is her faith. The character of the Church depends on the character of her faith. And, through the movement of the Reformation, the Church's life of faith received new depth and a force undreamed of. It is doubly true of the Church that she lives not by bread alone, but by every word which proceedeth out of the mouth of God. And the Word of God sounded forth once more. It went forth into all lands, calling to the nations with a tongue of brass, awakening their life, lifting up their hearts, and bringing forth fruit unto life eternal. Mounting ever higher, the spiritual movement goes on through the sixteenth century. It was so strong that it forced even Humanism into the background. The heart of the Church beat once more, and she also became whole. Not the Protestant Church only was reformed. In the battle over the great doctrinal questions, the opposite doctrine (whose aim was not to *abolish*, but to preserve the principles of the Middle Ages, and perfect them), attained a new religious force and clearness, as well as a great and reforming moral purpose. The fruit of the sixteenth century was schism, division between the

Protestant and Catholic Church—yet not schism alone, but the long-wished for, the fervently desired Reformation which with great tumult of spirit was finally accomplished. By the action and reaction of that movement which, kindled first of all in Germany, spread forth through all Christian lands, not only the Protestant Church, but the whole Church was reformed.

## § 37. *The Protestant Reformation*

The outward circumstance which called forth the action of Luther was the system of indulgences established by the Mediæval Church. Indulgence was originally a remission of the punishment inflicted by the Church. The Church's power to grant indulgences was afterwards extended to the temporal punishment of sins generally, and so to the temporal punishment which, according to the mediæval doctrine, was to be suffered in the other world in purgatory. Indulgence was granted in return for the performance of a good work. The Pope had the right to grant a general indulgence for the performance of certain specified works. Thus indulgences could be granted in return for money paid for any ecclesiastical purpose whatsoever. The idea was that, in granting indulgences, the Church offered, out of the treasure of superfluous good works (*tresaurus supererogationis*) which it possessed through the merits of Christ and the Saints, satisfaction to God in place of the penalty which the receiver of the indulgence would have had to pay.

In the year 1517, Pope Leo X. issued a general indulgence to the whole of Christendom. The money paid for it was to be used for the completion of the

Church of St. Peter's in Rome. Archbishop Albert of Mainz and Magdeburg was the Pope's agent for the sale of indulgences in one part of the German Empire. The half of the money collected in his dioceses fell to his share, in order that he might pay back to the house of Fugger the debt of thirty thousand gulden which he had had to borrow for the cost of his pallium. So those who sold indulgences on behalf of the Archbishop were accompanied by the agents of the house of Fugger, who took for themselves the half of the money as it was collected. The sale of indulgences assumed more and more the character of a traffic. It was looked upon in this light by contemporaries. The Elector Frederick of Saxony forbade the sale of indulgences in his territory, that his land might not be laid under contribution to pay for the pallium of Mainz. But the Elector could not hinder the activity of the Dominican monk Tetzel, the most zealous of the sellers of indulgences, and the most successful in the trade which he plied in the neighbourhood of the electoral territory of Saxony, within the domain of Magdeburg. Theoretically, in-dulgences were only to be granted in consideration of sincere penitence and contrition. But it was soon seen that this condition was taken easily by the seller of indulgences, and that the money-payment became the important thing. Thus Luther, at that time an Augustinian monk, professor of theology and pastor in Wittenberg, found that the penitents who confessed to him, and from whom he required true repentance and contrition, handed him their bills of indulgence as an equivalent. Luther felt that he was directly attacked in his pastoral ministry by the seller of indulgences. He even felt that he was injured by him in the most sacred of relations. Already, under the influence of those brethren of his Order who were akin to him in spirit, more especially under that of his superior, the Vicar-General John von Staupitz, he had learned that, according to the testimony of the Holy Scriptures, the inner change of heart which is brought about by lively faith is the sole and fully sufficient condition of justification, and the only one required by God. His whole religious nature recoiled from the profanation of holy things which he saw in the part played by the Dominican monk. He saw that 'Grace was bought for gold.' In the fire of his zeal he nailed his famous Ninety-five Theses on indulgences to the door of the Castle Church at Wittenberg. They were composed in Latin. According to the custom of the time they challenged all opponents to a learned controversy. They appealed first of all to the learned, and not to the multitude. Yet with one stroke they roused the whole people of Germany. They reasoned out the proposition that, though indulgence might be good and praiseworthy in itself, it could only absolve from punishment inflicted by the Church, not from punishment in the other world ; and that true penitence alone is required by God and alone sufficient in His eyes. 'To every Christian who is truly repentant there belongs full remission of punishment and guilt, without any letter of indulgence ;' the forgiveness of the Pope and his dispensation of the merits of Christ signified only a 'declaration of the divine forgiveness' (Theses, 36, 38). The shameful abuses, which were evident to all eyes in the proceedings of the sellers of indulgences, were opposed by an open and manly testimony, and by the clear proclamation of the Gospel of the grace of God.

In one week the Theses were spread through all
Germany. The monk and professor became the mouth-
piece of the nation. It was far from Luther's purpose
to attack either the Pope or the whole system of the
Church, or even to think of doing so. He thought
rather, that, 'if the Pope knew how the sellers of
indulgences flayed his flock, he would rather that St.
Peter's Church was burnt to ashes, than that it should
be built up out of the skin and bones of his sheep'
(Thesis, 50). He believed that he was defending the
opinion of the Pope against the sellers of indulgences.
But the battle which he had to fight for his convictions
forced him step by step further ; till he was in the end
obliged to recognize that the faith which he had created
for himself out of the Holy Scriptures, and which had
become to him the source and the strength of his life,
was in contradiction, not only to the whole system of
doctrine handed down from the Middle Ages, but to
the whole Church in its existing state.   In January
1519, at the request of the papal Ambassador Miltitz,
Luther made promise to keep silent, provided his
opponents would keep silent also. He had not yet
dreamed that he was called to be the reformer of the
Church. But his opponents did not keep silence. Dr.
Eck, a professor at Ingolstadt, had proposed to hold a
disputation at Leipsic with Karlstadt, a colleague of
Luther's at Wittenberg, in which certain propositions
which Luther had maintained were to be attacked.
Therewith Luther held himself absolved from his
promise. On the 4th of July 1519, he appeared face
to face with his opponent at Leipsic. The proceedings
began with a dispute concerning the papal authority.
Luther contended that the authority of the Pope was of

no divine origin, it was a merely human product of the development of history, like the authority of the German Emperor ; and belief in the papal authority was not necessary to salvation. Thus the decisive step was taken. His opponent reminded him that so Wiclif and John Huss had taught before, and that this same doctrine had been condemned by the great Council of Constance as a pestilent heresy. Luther's opinions were opposed by the authority of the Church : he would have to take his stand in opposition not only to the testimony of the papal decision, but to that of a General Council. And so he did. He declared that many of the propositions advanced by Huss were most Christian and evangelical ; that in matters of faith even a General Council lay open to correction through appeal to Scripture ; and that consequently even a General Council was capable of error. Thus did he break down the bridge between himself and the Mediæval Church. Henceforth from that moment to draw back was impossible. It became ever clearer to him that he must take up the battle, relying on the support of Scripture alone, against the formal authority of the Church which he had hitherto reverenced absolutely. In him conscience, faith, the private convictions of the individual, arose against a hierarchical organization. Many before him had already entered on the unequal conflict. Huss laid down his life as a martyr therein. Through Luther it was brought to a victorious end. The hour of the Present had struck. The individual appeared on the scene, in the convictions of his innermost heart prepared to yield to no external authority : to neither Emperor nor Pope, neither Bishop nor Council, but to the self-recognized truth of God alone. The individual desired an open path for the development of his inner freedom; that path was won for him, not by the classical culture of the Renaissance, but by the power of Christian faith in the truth of the Gospel, and by that alone. Taking his stand upon Holy Scripture and its eternal divine truth, the individual—in the person of Luther—found the moral energy and the force which urged him to the attack; it gave him power to take up the battle alone against a world, 'although that world were full of devils.' In the years which followed the disputation at Leipsic, Luther entered without disguise on the field of battle. He now saw before him the whole vast horizon of the Reformation. In the summer of 1520, there appeared, rousing all Christendom as with the blast of a trumpet, his great works, *To the Christian Nobles of the German Nation; On the Reform of the German State;* and *On the Babylonish Captivity of the Church.* To the papal Bull of excommunication (June the 16th, 1520) he replied, not only by burning it before the Elster gate in Wittenberg (December 10th, 1520), but notably with his treatise, addressed to the Pope, *On the Freedom of a Christian Man.* The universal priesthood of all believers, the direct relation of every Christian to God, the Christian's deliverance from sin and from all outward service of works,—these were the far-reaching thoughts with which he attacked and shattered the old system to its foundations. Luther then went to Worms in the year 1521, in order there to confess his belief before the Emperor and the assembled princes of the Empire, and to declare that he would only yield to reasons drawn from Holy Scripture (April the 17th and 18th). No ban of Pope or Emperor could hinder the work begun by him. The time of involuntary leisure spent at

Wartburg (from May 4th, 1521, till March 3rd, 1522) he employed in beginning his translation of the German Bible. (The New Testament was finished as early as 1522, the Old in 1534.) Even the revolutionary movements set on foot by the nobility of the Empire, under Franz von Sickingen (1523), and by the insurrectionary peasants (1525), movements which made the Gospel a pretext for worldly ambitions, even the iconoclastic and tumultuously subversive enterprises of the eccentric fanatics, Karlstadt and his comrades, could not hinder the progress of the Reformation.

In his address to the *Christian Nobles of the German Nation*, Luther had made it plain to the princes and States of the Empire that it was their right and their duty, founded on the universal priesthood of all believers, themselves to take in hand the reformation of the Church, if the proper organs of the Church, the Pope and bishops, refused to do so. That his undertaking had fallen upon a ready soil was shown by the Diet of Nürnberg, in 1522, when the States drew up a list of one hundred grievances against the See of Rome, against its ordinances and extortions, and declared that they would take means to right themselves if things were not changed. The Diet of Speier (1526) gave to the States, and with them to the barons and cities, freedom by imperial law to deal according to their conscience with the execution of the Edict of Worms, which ordered the outlawry of Luther and his followers. Thus was founded by imperial law the *jus reformandi* of the princes by which it lies in their hands to decide whether the Reformation shall be carried out in their dominions (*cujus regio, ejus religio*). Later on, in 1529, the Diet of Speier, cancelled by a retrograde movement the authority it had given to the imperial States, and thus required the strict execution of the Edict of Worms, which outlawed the heretics ; but it did so under protest of the imperial States that were in favour of the Reformation, a protest from which the evangelical States received their name of Protestant.    Consequently two parties arose in opposition to each other, one in favour of the innovation, the other against it.    At the Diet of Augsburg (1530) the Lutheran party presented their confession of faith, the *Confessio Augustana*, which became the standard under which Lutheranism has ever since fought.    By the Treaty of Schmalkalden in 1531 a military compact was afterwards made with the evangelical States.    The Articles of Schmalkalden (1537) were the final declaration of war against Rome, and the declaration of independence of the Protestant Church.    In the year 1546, the Emperor replied by the war of Schmalkalden, which led at first to the over-throw of Protestantism, but afterwards to its recognition by imperial law, owing to a change of party on the part of Duke Moritz of Saxony. (Treaty of Passau, 1552 ; Peace of Augsburg, 1555.) The Empire was turned into a neutral State, founded on the equal recognition of both confessions, the Catholic and the Evangelical—a result which, after the hard battles and the terrible misery of the Thirty Years' War, was finally confirmed by the Peace of Westphalia, in 1648.

Thus the Protestant Church was victorious in the hard struggle for existence.

The doctrine rested both upon the formal principle that Holy Scripture is alone binding as the rule of faith, and on the material principle of the justification of man through faith alone.    While, by the first principle, the doctrinal authority of the Church was cancelled (according to Protestant opinion, Church doctrine as such has no power binding on the conscience); by the second, the power of the priests and monks, with all that depended on it, was abolished.

### § 38. *The Constitution of the Protestant Church*

The original aim of the reformers was, not to establish a new organization, nor, speaking generally, a new basis for the Church. They meant to further develop and purify, not the constitution, but merely the doctrine of the Church ; and, if they could not succeed in winning the whole Church over to their persuasion, they were still willing to remain with their followers in the old Church, and to recognize the authority of Pope and bishops as an external authority ordained of men ; so long as they were permitted to preach the true Gospel and to administer the sacraments in a right sense. This is the standpoint taken by the Confession of Augsburg in the year 1530 (Article 28 to the end : 'Now it is not thought upon to take away the authority of the bishops, but it is asked and desired that they shall not force men's consciences to sin'). But it fell otherwise. In the Articles of Schmalkalden of 1537, the necessity of separation from the Church was already recognized, and obedience to the papal and episcopal authority was openly renounced. 'Seeing that the bishops are so devoted to the Pope as to defend godless doctrine and false worship, and that they will not suffer the ministry of pious preachers, but help the Pope to slay them, the churches have great and necessary cause why they should not recognize such as bishops' (*Art. Smalcald.*

*On the Authority and Supremacy of the Pope*).   A new constitution had to be made for the new Church.

But what sort of constitution?  'The two governments, spiritual and temporal, are not to be thrown together and mingled one with another' (*Confession of Augsburg*, Art. 28).   That is the underlying thought. To the Church belongs spiritual authority, and spiritual authority alone; to the State, temporal authority, and temporal authority alone.   Temporal authority is an external coercive authority; it 'guards with the sword and with bodily penalties the body, and not the soul, against external power.'   Spiritual authority, 'the power of the keys, or of the bishops,' that is, the authority of the Church, is no external coercive authority; it is 'an authority and command of God to preach the Gospel, to forgive and to retain sins, and to deliver and administer the Sacraments' (*Confession of Augsburg*, Art. 28).   Such 'authority of the Churches or of bishops' which 'giveth eternal good things' (through the administration of the Word and Sacraments) is to be 'used and carried out only by means of the ministry' (*Confession of Augsburg*, Art. 28).   This ministry belongs in its essence to every bishop and pastor equally and in the same manner; for, 'according to divine law, there is no difference between bishops and pastors or ministers' (*Art. Smalcald.*).   The Catholic distinction between bishops and pastors has 'arisen by human ordinance alone.'   Hence 'neither Peter, nor any other minister of the Word, may ascribe unto themselves any authority or supremacy over the churches'; for 'Paul teaches that the Church is more than the ministers'; that 'the keys (the spiritual authority) be not given unto one man alone, but to the whole Church'; and that

Christ 'delivers the highest and last judgment to the Church.' Therefore 'because the Gospel is yet persecuted by them who are ordained bishops, and honest persons scruple to suffer themselves to be ordained, every church has in this case authority and right to ordain ministers for itself' (*Art. Smalcald.*). Thus spiritual authority belongs to 'the Church,' that is, to all believers, and consequently to every assembly of believers, be it great or small ('where two or three are gathered together in My name, there am I in the midst of them'). But the Church exercises authority properly through the public ministry of the Word. Only in cases of necessity, if the holy office fails to fulfil its duty (for 'no power or authority is of higher value than the Word of God,' *Art. Smalcald.*), the power of the keys, that is, the spiritual authority, is exercised by 'the Church,' that is, by members of the community not *N* officially appointed to the ministry; 'so that, in need, even a layman may absolve another and act as his pastor.'

The ministry is at the same time the office of government in the Church, if only in virtue of the Church's sanction and commission. But the nature of this authority which it belongs to the ministry to exercise (that is, the power of the keys, or ecclesiastical authority), is purely spiritual; it is the authority to preach the Gospel, to administer the Sacraments, to excommunicate from the body of the Church, to ordain ministers; and all this, 'through the Word, without bodily power' (*Art. Smalcald.* ii.). External, coercive authority, formal and legal authority, which compels to subjection, is not included in the authority of the Church. The position of a temporal power would

thereby be given to the Church. The temporal
authority is coercive, legal authority. It must be its
care to help the Church in the exercise of her own
spiritual authority. 'But chiefly shall kings and princes,
as the chiefest members of the churches, help and see
to it that all manner of error be put away, and that
consciences be rightly instructed, as God has exhorted
kings and princes specially to such office.' 'For with
kings and great lords this shall be the chief care, that
they diligently further God's glory' (*Art. Smalcald.*).
The prince, as 'the chief member of the Church,' shall
place even his temporal authority in the service of the
Church. In what sense? In the sense that he shall
govern the Church himself? By no means. Ecclesiastical authority can only be exercised by the prince
(who as such is neither bishop nor pastor) in case of
need, if the regular ministry has forsaken its duty. In
this he stands on a complete equality with the other
members of the Church. But he shall turn his temporal
authority (for this alone he possesses) to the protection
of right doctrine and the prevention of 'such abomin-
able idolatry, and other countless vices.' What belongs
to the prince is the police-authority which we now call
'ecclesiastical supremacy' (*jus circa sacra*), that is,
such police-authority (so the prince's right of ecclesiastical supremacy was then understood) as includes superintendence both of the preaching and the defence of right
doctrine. The meaning of this police-authority of the
prince is rooted so deeply in the inner life of the Church
for this reason, that, according to the views of the
reformers, the Church as such renounces all claim to
coercive authority. Whatever legal coercive authority
is exercised in the Church belongs, therefore, not to

the Church, but to the temporal power. Even in the fifteenth century the *jus reformandi* of the prince (that is, extensive right of superintendence over doctrine and worship) was generally recognized as law. With this conviction Luther turned to the Christian Nobles of the German nation' (1520), and summoned them to the work of reformation. The princes' right of reform (*jus reformandi*) which was recognized as law, first in the Peace of Augsburg, and afterwards finally in the Peace of Westphalia, is the temporal authority with which the prince, as was shown above, is to serve the Church. It is not in itself an ecclesiastical authority, but only an authority auxiliary to the Church ; and yet an authority which, as the line between superintendence and government is a thin one, may at any moment be transformed into a governing authority. The same power of reform is possessed by the Catholic prince also in Catholic territory. But this in no way means that ecclesiastical authority belongs to him. It is just the same in Protestant countries. The Protestant prince possessed the same power of reform and no more. According to the views of the reformers, even the ideal of the Protestant Church is a self-governing organization, ruled by bishops, that is, by ministers, or, in cases of necessity, by the laity. Only, its instrument of government is the Word of God alone 'without bodily force.'

From these foundations has arisen the actual government of the Church by the prince. Luther never meant that the prince was to have the government of the Church. He meant him to have a merely spiritual office of superintendence over the minister ; and it was only in cases of necessity that the prince, like the rest of the laity, had the right to take upon himself the government of the Church.   But Luther's followers insisted on the establishment of coercive superintendence and government in the Church.   The Consistories or Episcopal Courts, which had possessed such authority, were to be re-established with the help of the prince.   And so, after Luther's death, it happened. The Sovereign Consistory to which the superintendents were subordinate, became the instrument of ecclesiastical government by the prince, and assumed the right of nomination and even of interdiction, both of which, according to reformed doctrine, belonged to the spiritual power ; so that the administration of the Word (in ordination and excommunication) was taken from the ministry ; and only the right of preaching the Word (which constituted the office of the ministry in the narrower sense) was left to it, together with the administration of the sacraments.   Why was this? Because the general community could not reach the ideal of the Reformers ; because mere spiritual authority (in the Reformers' sense, as explained above) was not sufficient to maintain Christian order in the community; because sin, indifference, and licentiousness required external restraint.   This is why temporal authority has become supreme in the Evangelical Church, and its right of superintendence has been turned into a right of government.   For according to the doctrine of the Reformers, external, legal, coercive authority belongs only to the State.   Because the Church was incapable of self-government through the Word of God alone, therefore the government of the Church fell to the prince as her helper in time of need.

Thus ecclesiastical government on the part of the prince is both in harmony and in contradiction with the fundamental ideas of the Reformation. In contradiction, so far as, according to the Reformation, the temporal authority is only to help, and not to govern the Church. In harmony, so far as, according to the opinions of the Reformers, legal authority is never to be exercised by the Church, but even in the Church by the State alone. When and so far as ecclesiastical authority becomes legal authority, it must be transformed from a spiritual authority (belonging to the Church) to a political authority (belonging to the State).

These thoughts appear somewhat strange to us to-day. They are certainly not modern. But there is a grand idealism in them, born of the Christian faith, which, if its immediate result was the establishment of a succession of individual national churches, outwardly separate and governed each by its own sovereign, is nevertheless an idealism which will never cease to give to the Evangelical Church a type to be striven after, and a spur to further development.

## § 39. *The Lutherans and the Reformed Churches*

Luther was the first great herald of the Reformation ; but he was not the only man who determined the character of its progress. Side by side with him stood Melanchthon, the refined scholar and theologian whose humanism went far to compensate for much of Luther's hardness, and who became the creator of the Protestant system of education (*Præceptor Germaniæ*), and of Protestant scientific theology. Opposed to Luther stood the great men who became the leaders of the reformed Protestant Reformation.

In Switzerland Ulrich von Zwingli appeared as a reformer at about the same time as Luther. The study of the Holy Scriptures had led him, like Luther, into opposition to many of the doctrines of the Church. In 1518, he preached in Maria-Einsiedeln, a celebrated resort of pilgrims, against pilgrimages and the sale of indulgences. In 1519, as a preacher in the great church of Zürich, he soon swayed the city and its government by means of his preaching, and effected in a few years the completion of the Reformation. He started, not like Luther, from the religious needs of man's nature, but from the more purely intellectual side, from knowledge, coloured by his humanistic culture. Hence the distaste of the Zwinglian reformers for mysticism. The outward forms of worship were simplified as much as possible, and all images banished from the Church ; the plain Word alone was to be left. In his doctrine of the Lord's Supper Zwingli was opposed not only to the Catholic doctrine of Transubstantiation, but also to the Lutheran doctrine that the true body and the true blood of Christ are received by the partakers (both faithful and unfaithful) of the Lord's Supper, in and together with the bread and wine. According to Zwingli, the Lord's Supper is a memorial of the Lord. With regard to this doctrine Luther and Zwingli are irreconcilably opposed. In all other matters agreement seemed possible, but not in this. The religious conference at Marburg in October 1529 at which Luther and Zwingli met in person, ended by confirming this division. This schism afterwards divided the Reformation. The opposition was evident as early as the Diet of Augsburg in 1530. Four cities of Upper Germany, Strasburg, Constance,

Memmingen, and Lindau, refused to subscribe to the
Confession of Augsburg on account of the doctrine
of the Lord's Supper, and presented to the Emperor
a confession of their own, known as the Tetrapolitana,
which, however, the Emperor refused to receive. Zwingli
died upon the battlefield of Kappel (1531), in the
defence of his faith against the Catholic cantons. His
work was continued, and made historically important
by Calvin, for Calvin gave a fixed form to the doctrine
of the French Reformed Church in Geneva; and thence,
by means of his numerous disciples a way was opened
to it in France and the Netherlands, and before all,
by John Knox in Scotland, whence it has exerted a
powerful influence on the Church of England and the
New World.

The characteristics of Calvin's Reformation were its
doctrine of Predestination, and the Puritan rigour of
its Church discipline. In his doctrine of the Lord's
Supper he took a mediating position between Luther
and Zwingli. According to Calvin, the mere bread
and wine are indeed received by the mouth; and
nevertheless, the glorified body of Christ is spiritually
received, but only by the faithful partakers of the
Lord's Supper.

In Germany also, especially in Hesse and the Palati-
nate, the reformed doctrine became widespread. The
*Catechism of Heidelberg* (1563) is one of the most
important statements of the reformed confession; yet
so-called Calvinistic church-discipline, in its full rigour,
never took root in Germany.

The division of the Protestants into the Lutheran
and Reformed Churches was for the cause of the
Reformation a misfortune never sufficiently to be

deplored. It broke the force of the reform movement;
it raised endless contests which were sometimes hateful
in the extreme; and it gave the enemies of the Gospel
fresh courage and strength for resistance. Nevertheless,
that division is not only the necessary expression of
the individualism involved in Protestantism, but it has
been a source of rich blessing. The great struggle
for the truth of the Gospel found utterance in two
distinct forms, and from the Reformation there arose
two great ecclesiastical currents which were one at
their source, and yet each had its own especial powers
and gifts of grace. The historical problem and service
of Lutheran Protestantism was before all things to
sink itself, as it were, in the depths of divine doctrine,
in the mysteries of Christ's person and His work; while
to the Reformed Church it was given to spread abroad
the Gospel far over the Roman and the Anglo-American
world, and to bring its organizing force to bear upon
the practical life of the individual Christian, as well
as of the Church. There was a fervour of religious
life, a power for world-wide work in shaping history,
in the iron Puritanism of the Scotch Church, which
in such a form could only have grown upon the soil of
the reformed faith. And in the Reformed Church grew
up that Presbyterian and Synodal form of ecclesiastical
constitution which gave the community an orderly
share in the government of the Church, and thus
fulfilled our ideal of the Lutheran Reformation. The
conflict of the two Protestant confessions with one
another may have been ruinous; not without blessing
has been their mutual influence, through mutual participation in each other's gifts.

# CHAPTER II

## COUNTER REFORMATION

### § 40. *The Catholic Reformation*

THE spiritual forces which had brought forth and
sustained the Mediæval Church were by no means √
destroyed in the sixteenth century. They were only
checked by the new movement of reform. Nay more,
they too could satisfy themselves and gain new life
through the new spirit brought forth by the Protestant
Reformation. In requiring reformation of the Church
in head and members, they were all at one who in the
fifteenth and sixteenth centuries had the interests of
the Church at heart. Difference of opinion arose only
on the question how far this reformation should go, and
what portions of the Church's life it should be allowed
to touch. The reformation of doctrine, from which
Luther, Zwingli, and Calvin started was given up by
this party; and a mere reformation of discipline of
the life and organization of the Church was demanded.
But it was nevertheless the storm of the spiritual
movement raised by means of the Protestant reformation of doctrine, and the great conflict of religious
opinions kindled thereby, which made reform possible,
even in this narrower sense. Nay more, the Protestant
movement, started on the ground of church doctrine,
necessarily called forth, by way of reaction, a more

definite, a clearer and fuller statement of the opposite doctrine ; so that the Catholics also came forward with their series of dogmatic propositions, all newly formulated.   In this sense even they had a reform of dogma, which, because it was a spiritual reform, brought forth new religious forces, and opened out, even for them, a new path of development.   Thus, in opposition to the Protestant Reformation, arose a Catholic Reformation, known as the Counter-Reformation.   While the Protestant Reformation fills the first half of the sixteenth century, and is the ruling power in it, the Catholic Counter-Reformation begins about the middle of the century.   It revived more and more effectually the forces of the traditional Mediæval Church, and rallied them more and more around her ; until, by means both of its conflict and of its involuntary association with Protestantism, it brought forth the modern Catholic Church.

The two powers, by means of which the Catholic Reformation was brought about, were the Order of Jesuits and the Council of Trent.

## § 41.  *The Order of Jesuits*

The Order of Jesuits is a product of Spanish Catholicism.   In Spain all through the Middle Ages national and religious enthusiasm were mingled in the fierce battle with the Moors.   Mediæval Catholicism had there preserved a degree of warmth and of religious force which it lacked in other parts of the Church. Spain sprang up, as it were in a single night, as the ruling power of the old and the new worlds.   Just as the Spanish kingdom took the lead in the development of absolute monarchy, so Spanish Catholicism was foremost in restoring the Church's unlimited authority to teach doctrine. A Spanish noble, Ignatius Loyola, founded in 1534 the Order of Jesuits (confirmed by Pope Paul III. in 1540), with the view of raising up for Jesus Christ, the Head of the Church, and for the Pope, His visible representative, an army of absolutely devoted soldiers, to overcome not only unbelief among the heathen, but the unbelief which had arisen in the bosom of the Church herself. To the three oaths of poverty, chastity, and obedience, hitherto taken by the Monastic Orders, a fourth was added, the oath of absolute obedience to the Pope. The Jesuits gave the foremost place to the duty of obedience (which the old Orders regarded but as a means to an end), that the highest aim of their Order might be attained—the perfecting of a power to be used in the service of the Papacy, the development of a determined unrelenting Catholicism.

The ideal of the Order of Jesuits (the 'Society of Jesus') is that of absolute military subordination, even in the sphere of spiritual life. This object is attained, first, by the isolation of the individual—the Jesuit is to know neither friends nor kindred. All closer relations, even those of the individual members of the Order among themselves, are forbidden, that the Superior may have sole influence and authority over them. Secondly, by the strict surveillance of the individual, by means of an elaborate system of espionage and informing, and by means of the duty laid upon the Order to confess everything to the Superior, even the most secret feelings. Finally, by spiritual exercises (*exercitia spiritualia*), a sort of spiritual drill, which, elaborated as it was in masterly fashion by the founder of the Order, revealed more and more to the eyes of the drill-sergeant the true condition of the souls under his care; at the same time it induced in them a state of spiritual exaltation and emotion which gave them full command over themselves, and which fitted them not only to command others, but, in their turn, unconditionally and unhesitatingly, to subject themselves to another. This principle of subordination was summed up in the axiom that every member of the Order is pledged to see and acknowledge Christ Himself in the person of his Superior. The crown of moral personality —freedom of private moral judgment—is thus thrown aside. Subjection to an external opinion is regarded as the true moral perfection. It is a degradation, a suppression, an annihilation of the most precious gift given to man. The ultimate consequences of Monasticism are to be seen here: complete ascetism requires the destruction of the will also. The Order of Jesuits is the most perfect type of that principle to which the Protestant spirit, and also the common moral consciousness of the present age, is most absolutely opposed. But as the Protestant principle—the freedom of the private conscience from all human authority—has its followers, the opposite principle—the subjection of the whole life of the individual, and even of the conscience, to a visible authority—has its followers also; and just in this straining of the principle of authority, the extreme consequences of which are subversive of all morality, lies the secret of the remarkable power to which Jesuitism, and consequently modern Catholicism, owes its success.

The Order of Jesuits was bound to regard Protestantism as the born foe to whose destruction it was

called.   Its aim was first of all to effect an intellectual
reaction against the strong and stormy progress of the
Reformation.   German Catholicism was unequal to the
task.   Protestant doctrine made its way almost un-
resisted through the whole of Germany, and penetrated
even to Bavaria and Austria.   The universities, the
schools, the clergy, and the monks who still remained
true to the old faith, were far from making any complete
hearty resistance to the new preaching of the Gospel.
They were themselves inwardly stirred by the new
doctrine, more doubtful and uncertain than persuaded
of the living power of the contrary belief.   These
relations were first changed when the Jesuits came
over to Germany in the first half of the sixteenth
century.   The 'Spanish priests,' as the Jesuits were
popularly called, gave from the pulpit and the teachers'
chair a new utterance to the Catholic faith.   Their aim
was to defeat Protestantism with Protestant weapons.
Mediæval Scholasticism, which was the learning of the
Dominicans, had given place to Humanism, which made
common cause with Protestantism.   The Jesuits made
humanistic learning and culture their own, in order to
turn it to the service of the Church.   In opposition to
the schools of Protestant learning, arose the schools of
the Jesuits ; side by side with Protestant science, a
Jesuitical science, furnished with all possible resources ;
side by side with Protestant preaching, the preaching of
the Jesuits, equally delivered in the language of the
people, equally founded on the Bible, and which spread
Catholicism far and wide.   The Jesuits brought the
whole strength of their intellectual and moral forces
to bear on the single object of annihilating Protestantism
with its own weapons.

But this literary and purely intellectual reaction did not lead the Jesuits speedily enough to the goal. External means had also to be applied and authoritative measures taken in the service of the Church. Thus in the second half of the sixteenth century, owing to the activity of the Jesuits, there began the violent reformation—the Counter-Reformation strictly so called. In Germany the Treaty of Augsburg of 1555 (by which every prince had power to decide the religious confession of his own territory) gave the legal grounds for the movement. The Counter-Reformation began in Bavaria at the instigation of the Jesuits who had been settled there since 1556,—with Ingolstadt as their head-quarters. In 1563 all evangelical priests and laymen were driven from Bavaria, and the evangelical nobles excluded from the Diet. The spiritual princes followed the example so given; in Trier, Wurzburg, Bamberg, and Salzburg, Protestant ministers were replaced by pupils of the Jesuits, so that all preaching of the reformed doctrine was put down. In 1598 by a decree of the Archduke Ferdinand, a pupil of the Jesuits, the Lutheran ministers were driven out of Styria, Carinthia, and Carniola. What was done in Germany was done also elsewhere. The bloodthirsty government of the Catholic Queen Mary of England (1553-1558); of the Spanish Duke of Alva in the Netherlands (1567); the Massacre of St. Bartholomew in France (1572) were so many terrible memorials of the Counter-Reformation, which was guided and completed by the spirit of Jesuitism. In Germany also the movement finally led to that intolerable strife which ended later in the bloodshed and misery of the Thirty Years' War. That strife was closed by the Peace of Westphalia (1648), by which Protestantism once for all received legal recognition. In consequence of the Counter-Reformation it had suffered irreparable losses in the territories ruled by Catholic princes, especially in Bavaria and Austria. Whereas in the middle of the sixteenth century it was already in a way to conquer all Germany, it was now repressed and confined within certain definite limits. Yet it had preserved its existence even in Germany, and there Protestantism stands to this day opposed to Jesuitism, hindering its supremacy even within the Catholic Church itself.

The Pope protested against the Peace of Westphalia and declared it invalid, like the Peace of Augsburg before it. But his words echoed vainly and unheard. It was the first time for a long period that a great political act had taken place without the co-operation, nay more, in spite of the opposition of the Pope. Times had changed. The Middle Ages had gone by. The temporal sword of the Pope was broken. Protestantism had attained a twofold object in spite of the Jesuits: it had not only maintained itself, but it had changed the aspect of the whole political world, by the destruction of the temporal supremacy of the Papacy.

## § 42. *The Council of Trent*

The Catholic Reformation found formal expression and completion in the Council of Trent, which, with many interruptions, was assembled at Trent during the years 1545-1562. By this Council, in agreement with Mediæval Scholasticism, the dogma of tradition, that is, of the binding power of church doctrine, as well as the dogmas of original sin, the seven sacraments, transubstantiation, penance, and extreme unction, the Host, the consecration of priests and of the hierarchy, the sacrament of holy matrimony, purgatory, the worship of saints and relics, monastic vows, etc., were maintained in their anti-Protestant sense. What had hitherto been merely matter of scientific, that is, of scholastic, doctrinal opinion, which might have been prevalent, but could hardly have been considered binding in point of law, was now established as the doctrinal law of the Church, legally binding upon all. Modern Catholic dogma, for the first time expressed in definite terms, now arose in opposition to the Protestant doctrinal movement. The Protestant principle of the authority of Holy Scripture as the sole rule of faith was clearly and deliberately confronted with the Catholic axiom of the authority of the Church, of its authority to decide these very questions of dogma. To the Catholic his Church is the object and the source of his faith. To believe in this visible Church, in its holiness and infallibility, to believe that alone which the Church teaches, is to be a Catholic. The principle of authority, the authority of the Church commanding the conscience and the faith of the individual, was expressed in unmistakable terms as the essence of the Catholic faith, newly confirmed by the Council of Trent. All other doctrinal decisions were included in this principle as deductions from it. The re-establishment of dogma was accompanied by a reformation of the constitution and discipline of the Church. Many of the most crying abuses were put down; the perversion of indulgences as a source of gain was forbidden (from this time the sale of indulgences ceased), the clergy were pledged to the personal administration of their office, and so forth. The main point was that

the Papacy and the clergy were filled with a new spirit. *N*
The corrupt and worldly-minded Papacy which had
flourished in the fifteenth and the beginning of the
sixteenth century disappeared as by a miracle. As
soon as it took in hand the work of reform, the Papacy
set itself more and more clearly at the head of the
vigorously ecclesiastical party. Through its conflict
with Protestantism it had come to itself again. And,
as it fared with the Papacy, so it fared with the Catholic
clergy. The sixteenth century movement of reform
was a universal one. The reformed Protestant Church
was confronted by a reformed Catholic Church.

# DIVISION IV

# PIETISM AND THE ILLUMINATION

## § 43. *Pietism*

THE great conflict of the age of the Reformation, with
its battle for the Gospel of justification by faith, brought
forth two great movements, which, now advancing side
by side, now conflicting with each other, ruled the
following age from the end of the sixteenth to the first
half of the eighteenth century.

The one movement aimed at elaborating a system of
doctrine which should give a scientific form to the
substance of the evangelical truth so lately recognized,
and thus bring it within the full comprehension of the
Church. This was the ruling tendency in the Lutheran
Church. It was a continuation of the work already
begun by Melanchthon. It produced the dogmatic
Lutheranism of the seventeenth century, and created a
Lutheran theology which found its most significant
expression in the celebrated works of Johann Gerhard
(Professor of theology at Jena from the year 1616;
died 1637), whose influence extended over the whole
field of Protestantism. There was, however, a danger
in this development of a system of theological doctrine,
the danger of more or less neglecting for subtle
questions of dogma, the real, quickening truths of salva-

tion ; and in this way of forcing the minute refinements of doctrinal theology upon the Church as law.  But the Church can only live by the true, plain Word of God ; not by the uncertain results of human theological learning.  And it was clear that the Lutheran Church did not wholly escape this danger.  The Formula of Concord of 1577, though it found only partial acceptance in Lutheran countries, tended very decidedly in this direction.  While the Confession of Augsburg in 1530, and the Articles of Schmalkalden in 1537, are merely a powerful expression of those truths upon which evangelical faith depends, already in the Formula of Concord the *Epigoni* are the leaders, with whom controversial theology comes to the front, and rules not only the science but the very life of the Church by logical conclusions.  But Lutheran theology of the seventeenth century moved in the lines marked out for it by the Formula of Concord, and exerted its powerful influence on the Church in the spirit of that formula.  Such a movement was essentially one of the subtlest dogmatism , and its fruit, as Lutheran theologians of that time have themselves testified,[1] was a new Scholasticism, an outward ecclesiasticism which disowned the inner power of Christianity.  The natural tendency of this movement was opposed to the reformed doctrine; and if Lutheran theology was right in defending the Lutheran confession, it was equally wrong when tempted to exaggerate the opposition, and in the interest of dogma to set up its own body of doctrine above the substance of Holy Scripture.  The one - sided dogmatism of Lutheran theology in that age was almost as successful as Roman

---

[1] *E.g.* Johann Arndt, still famous for his religious writings ; died at Celle in 1621.

*solved*

Catholicism itself in blinding the eyes of the people to the power of the clear word of Scripture, by throwing the doctrine of the Church into a scholastic form. But the Lutheran Church bore within it the power to free itself from such excrescences; and, besides bringing forth that dogmatic movement, it gave life and energy to the forces which were best able to counterbalance it.

The second movement which arose from the Reformation, aimed, first of all, not at doctrine, but at the practical formation and realization of the Christian life. It began in the Reformed Church, and this chiefly through the influence of Calvin. It brought forth the Puritan force and vigour of the French and the Anglo-Scotch or Presbyterian Reformed Churches. At the same time, by means of its synods and its presbyterian constitution, it was able to give the people a share in the life of the Church; and this was a safeguard against the torpidity into which the Lutheran congregations, under the ecclesiastical government of the territorial sovereign and the orthodox theologians, too often fell.

*legal*

But Calvinistic Puritanism involved also a legalism, a government of external discipline, which destroyed the freedom of Christian men, and was a blow to its evangelicalism. And even here, if we consider the history of the Churches of England, Scotland, and the Netherlands, there arose a dogmatism, a dependence on single articles of faith for which no proof could be given other than the doctrine of the Church; it was a dogmatism which in hatred of every shortcoming, and in overbearing self-righteousness in no degree came behind that of contemporary Lutheran theologians. The spirit of the monks and of the schoolmen appeared to have gathered new strength in the field of Protestantism.

Yet, in still greater strength, the true spirit of the Gospel remained in the Evangelical Churches, both of the Lutheran and the Reformed Confessions. An inward reaction began which delivered the Protestant Church from the dangers of a one-sided development.

This movement, which is now known by the name of Pietism, began in the Reformed Church. In the Church of Holland (at first under the leadership of Labadie, somewhere about the year 1660), then in other territory of the Reformed Church, was formed the sect of 'The Regenerate,' which was indifferent to questions of dogma as such, and strove after practical Christianity manifested in an ascetic life, and in a mystic devotion to the bridegroom, Christ. In this the dogmatism of reformed Puritanism was abandoned, and a new expression given to the characteristic endeavour of the Reformed Church to realize the Christian ideal of life. Yet in this movement it was the Lutheran Church that triumphed. This was the meaning of the essentially Lutheran Pietism of Spener and Francke, which arose in opposition to dogmatism at the end of the seventeenth century. Spener (born at Rappolsweiler in Alsace, in 1635) united in himself the influence of the reformed tendency to a vigorous and almost ascetic Christian life (he lived some time in Geneva when a student), and the Lutheran tendency to the purely scriptural doctrine of the Bible. It was the time when, principally through Spener's master, Professor Sebastian Schmidt of Strasburg,[2] the earnest study of the Bible Text, with a view to its interpretation, was revived in the Lutheran Church. It was also the time when all spirits were cast down by the misery

[1] For an account of these theologians, cf. W. Horning, *Dr. Sebastian Schmidt of Strasburg*, 1885.

of the Great War, and were ready to receive the con-
solation offered by the Christian revelation of salvation;
when Paul Gerhardt lifted up his clear, sweet voice, and
gave to the living experience of Christian faith the rare
and genuinely poetic expression that goes straight to
the heart; when a number of Lutheran theologians,
like Grossbauer (died at Rostock in 1661) and others,
had already arisen to further by their unhesitating
witness the still living spirit of true evangelical Lutheranism, and to give utterance to the longing after inward
regeneration of the life of faith, actuated by the power
of the Spirit. Spener was the leader of the whole
movement; and he crowned its victory when, in his
*Pia Desideria* (1675), he advocated with impressive
earnestness the institution of private meetings for the
common study of the Bible, the participation of the laity
in the affairs of the Church, and the realization of
Christian faith in a life of love; when, above all, in his
religious and biblical studies (published after 1670), he
made a way for a method of scriptural interpretation
which treated the Bible, not as a source of scholastic
controversies, but as a power of life unto life. Once
more the first place was given to the Bible above the
Confession of the Church. The demand for regeneration through faith sounded through the Protestant world
like a mighty trumpet-call, and the magnificent institutions founded in Halle by Francke (the foundation-
stone of the Orphanage was laid in 1695) were an
imperishable witness to the practical power of genuine
Christian love, united with a trust in God as genuine
and absolute. Pietism exercised a decisive influence
on the Moravian Church of Count Zinzendorf (founded
as an independent, free, Christian Society in 1727), and

through the Moravians on the Methodists likewise. The Methodists in England, and even more in the New World, represented the Reformed Church in a newly revived form, distinguished by its insistence on personal sanctification. (The first Methodist society was founded by John Wesley, in London, in the year 1739.) But the chief glory of Pietism is this: that by its means the great Protestant missions were set on foot. The first Lutheran missionaries, Ziegenbalg and others, came from the Orphanage founded by Francke at Halle. Protestantism reached the height of its mature strength when it stirred up its emissaries, and sent them forth into the world to win it over to the Gospel of Christ.

The new movement could not fail to produce outgrowths. The weakness of Pietism lay in its Separatism and in its Methodism. In its Separatism, so far as it fostered the tendency of narrow societies of 'truly awakened' thinkers to cut themselves off from the 'great masses,' to form *ecclesiolæ in ecclesia*, and thus to weaken the power and meaning of Church organization. In its Methodism, so far as it prescribed a 'method,' which, although not so harsh as the Methodism peculiar to England and North America, was at any rate akin to it, and which was meant to lead to the 'breaking forth of Grace in man,' and thus to regeneration, by artificially arousing the sense of penitence. This view resulted in the formation of a detailed canon of morality which demanded as a proof of assured salvation the renunciation of the world, the renunciation of some of the pleasures of life which are perfectly allowable in themselves (such as dancing, playing cards, going to theatres, etc.); so that the principle of justification by works appeared once more in the very midst of Pro-

testantism.    Owing to these exaggerations, Pietism fell
into that disfavour which already about the middle of
the eighteenth century robbed it of all further influence
on Protestant society ; while, about this time, another
great movement, the Illumination, arose and led the
world into new paths.   Nay more, Pietism itself, by
setting free the individual from the organization and
doctrine of the Church, prepared the way for the triumph
of the Illumination, and consequently for its own dissolution.

Nevertheless, the result of Pietism is indestructible.
Throughout the age of the Illumination, until the nineteenth century, it remained the one power which truly
preserved the evangelical Christian life, albeit amongst
a small minority, until with the opening of our century
the hour had come for the regeneration of the Evangelical Church.   Up to our own day it represents a
form of Protestantism which, together with the great
confessional movement of our time, may be regarded
as the complement of that movement, and equally
necessary for the life of the Protestant Church.   In the
one movement it is mainly doctrine, in the other mainly
life in the Gospel sense, in which the spiritual forces
active in both tendencies find their goal, and through
which they have any meaning in the history of the
Church.   Neither movement has full power of healthy
development without the other.   Individuals will in-
cline either to the one or to the other—this is only
human nature—but the Church can dispense with
neither.   United, they represent and rule the Protestant
Church of the present.

The Pietism of the end of the seventeenth and the
beginning of the eighteenth centuries was the last great

surge of the waves of the ecclesiastical movement begun
by the Reformation; it was the completion and the
final form of the Protestantism created by the Reformation. Then came a time when another intellectual
power henceforth took possession of the minds of men.

## § 44. *The Illumination*

All Western Europe until the end of the seventeenth
century was dominated by the ecclesiastical development
which culminated in the Reformation and the Counter-
Reformation. After that time another spirit began to
be felt.

By the discoveries made in physical science in the
sixteenth and seventeenth centuries, together with the
philosophical movement to which they gave rise, more
especially in England, the way was prepared for a new
theory of the universe which sought its standpoint, not
in the faith of the Church, but in what is made known
through human reason. With boldness and determination men set about the work of deliverance from the
power of tradition; and the materials handed down by
history were subjected to a process of criticism by which
all that was historical, relative, and accidental was to
be separated from that which is eternal, rational, and
inherent in human nature and in the nature of things.
A natural law, a natural State, a natural society, and
a natural religion shone as the great ideals on the
intellectual horizon, and carried away the world of the
eighteenth century in a movement of passionate endeavour. These battles prepared the way for the rise
of modern humanity.

Traditional Christianity also was subjected to criticism,

from the standpoint of its agreement with reason and nature; and neither the Catholic nor the Protestant form of Christianity could satisfy the demands of philosophy for a system conformable to reason. This was natural; for religion springs from the relation of man to God, whose being evidently and necessarily transcends the human understanding and its forms of thought. Religion *must* end in the incomprehensible; and the power which makes it religion, the power which satisfies the soul and frees it from the stress of earthly things, the power which perfects both the nation and the individual life belongs to religion by virtue, not of the comprehensible, but of the incomprehensible in it which transcends human thought and understanding; the power of religion lies in the mystery through which it leads to God, the incomprehensible Being whom the understanding cannot reach.

The eighteenth century sought after a religion which should unite two contradictory things; which should satisfy both the understanding and the desire of the soul for the eternal, the infinite, the incomprehensible. The result of the movement was a confession of faith which acknowledged only the three great objects: God, virtue, and immortality. Every positive element of the Christian faith was rejected; yet a consistent series of truths which could be proved by reason was never reached. The only result was that the firm staff of Christian faith, the only sure support in the way through life, was turned into a bruised reed, and faith itself into vague ideas which awakened doubt. In the second half of the eighteenth century Rationalism was victorious along the whole line. It ruled both in the Protestant and the Catholic Church. Defended by

Voltaire and Lessing with the weapons of ridicule and
of penetrating sagacity, it developed its highest product
in the philosophy of Kant, where the limits of the
human understanding are laid down, and both the
existence of God and the immortality of the soul are
declared to be unprovable postulates of the moral or
practical reason.  Kant's philosophy signified the completion and the self-destruction of Rationalism ; it was
the attainment of a summit of development from which
there was suddenly opened a view into an altogether
new and unlooked-for land.  Reason was once more
shown its limits ; and philosophy itself had recognized
that religion is not meant for a sort of philosophical
doctrine satisfying the need of the understanding for
knowledge, but rather for an immediate power, con-
vincing men without logical proof and satisfying both
the need of the will for deliverance from the world and
sin, and the need of man for God.  Yet Kant remained
in the bonds of Rationalism when he made mere morality,
the ' recognition of our duties as divine commands,' the
end and aim of religion.   The sovereign power in which,
according to Kant, the moral law appears as the
unconditional, ' categorical imperative' (binding by virtue
of its content alone, and not by virtue of any principle
of means to an end), offers a very imperfect compensation
for the fact that God is transformed once more into the
angry lawgiver of Sinai, and that there is no place in
Kant's system for the ' Word of God ' who has revealed
Himself to the world ' full of grace and truth.'

The great practical results of the Illumination were
the destruction of the Jesuit Order, the foundation of
the omnipotent authority of the State, and the idea of
Toleration.

## § 45. *The Destruction of the Jesuit Order*

The Jesuit Order had already prepared the way for its fall through its own development. The morality it preached had become casuistry which sought but the cases in which evil could be done with a good conscience. Here are instances of such cases, when the inward intention is directed, not to the sin as such, but to some ulterior object which may be altogether praiseworthy (*methodus dirigendae intentionis*); or when for some good purpose a narrower meaning or a secret condition is mentally attached to a promise given (mental reservation); or when use is made of some ambiguous expression (amphiboly). In these doctrines the proposition that the end justifies the means is not directly expressed, but it is implied. Nay more, the Jesuit moralists and theologians represented the requirements of morality as mere matter of opinion; they developed the doctrine that a man may even act against his own conscience, if he only has on his side a 'probable opinion,' that is to say, the testimony of some writer recognized as an authority. This is the doctrine known as Probabilism. It was first scientifically developed by a Spanish Dominican, Bartolomé de Medina, in 1577, and was afterwards carried further and brought to its perfection by other Jesuit writers, such as the Spaniard Escobar (died 1633). By means of this doctrine of Probabilism the door was thrown open to every kind of immorality. The Papacy itself, however it may have tried to protect the Jesuits as its truest followers, was obliged to make a stand against Jesuit morality. Alexander VII. in 1655 refused to sanction Probabilism and the doctrines connected with it; Innocent XI.

solemnly issued bills condemning sixty-five of the laxer moral axioms of the Jesuits (1679). The Order was obliged in 1687 to repudiate its connection with Probabilism by the formal declaration that it would not hinder the advancement of doctrine opposed thereto. Nevertheless, within the Order itself the most decided resistance was offered to all other doctrine by its General Gonzalez (1687 till 1705), who had been elected by Pope Innocent VII. on account of his supposed hostility to Probabilism ; and the Order never applied the enormous power which it pos-sessed over its members to put down a moral doctrine which was defended principally by Jesuit writers them-selves.

The Jesuit Order met with a powerful opponent in Jansenism, a tendency which began in the University of Louvain (where Jansen was professor from 1630 till 1636), and then became widespread, especially in France. The Jesuit Order represented the doctrine received by the Catholic Church : that by virtue of the freedom which remains to him in spite of the Fall, man is able by his own works (aided by the divine grace) to co-operate in his own salvation (semi-Pelagianism) ; whereas Jansenism, like the Protestant reformers, de-fended the Augustinian doctrine : that the salvation of the elect is solely owing to the grace of God which predestines one to salvation, and another to damnation. Jansenism, as was only natural, was repeatedly con-demned by the Pope. It was an attempt at reformation made within the Catholic Church, in opposition to Jesuitism. It owed its popularity chiefly to the moral earnestness of its followers, an earnestness which amounted to ascetic rigour ; and before long they found a local centre in the Cistercian convent of Port Royal in the neighbourhood of Versailles.

The influence of Jansenism on the world's history consists, not so much in its dogmatic teaching, as in the criticism which it applied to the morality of the Jesuits. Jansenism was directly opposed to the moral principles of the Jesuits, and was moreover involved in a doctrinal controversy with the Order which was a battle for life or death. Therefore from the ranks of the Jansenists came the strongest reaction against Jesuit morality. To their sect belonged Blaise Pascal, the celebrated mathematician and natural philosopher, whose *Lettres Provinciales* (published 1656-57) were the most complete and the most powerful, as well as the wittiest expression of the general indignation aroused by Jesuit morality. In the Catholic Church itself Jansenism was naturally overpowered by Jesuitism, which defended the official dogmas of that Church. Nevertheless, the Jesuits found that Pascal's attack, sparkling with wit and intellect and scorn, was invulnerable. More than sixty editions of the *Lettres Provinciales* were circulated. They struck at the powerful Order the first great blow which permanently shattered its position. In attacking its morality they hit the Achilles' heel of Jesuitism.

Besides this, the Order became even more completely absorbed in the worldly interests of power and wealth; all that was spiritual in it was stifled by its great commercial undertakings and financial enterprises. Yet again, the Jesuit doctrine which under certain conditions (that is to say, in the interests of the Church) sanctioned the murder of princes, a doctrine, which, for instance, gave the dagger into the hands of the murderers of Henry III. and Henry IV. of France, naturally aroused anger and repulsion against the Order.   But the decisive event by which it was finally overthrown was the spread of the Illumination in the eighteenth century.   To the eighteenth century, which was filled with the spirit of philosophy and of free discovery, the Jesuit Order appeared as an anachronism of the most offensive kind. It was as a spirit of darkness, bearing with it the scholasticism and the intellectual barbarism of the Middle Ages, that the spirit of Jesuitism confronted the eighteenth century.   The Church itself, both Catholic and Protestant, began to appropriate the ideas of the Illumination, which rejected the essentially Christian element in religion and held fast by its universally human side alone, as the true kernel of Christianity. The Jesuit Order alone remained standing, paying homage to the extremest Catholicism, a monument of spiritual tendencies long since passed away.   The whole culture of the eighteenth century rose up against that Order.

Thus the hour of its fall had come.   When required by the King of France to take measures for the reform of the Order, their General, Ricci, returned his famous answer : '*Sint ut sunt, aut non sint*' ('They must be as they are or not at all').   The issue was decided in conflict with the State, which saw the Jesuit Order opposed to it as a State within the State.   The Order was abolished in 1759 in Portugal ; in 1764 in France ; and in 1767 in Spain and Naples.   Finally in 1773, Clement XVI., yielding to the combined pressure of the Government and the tendency of the age, abolished it from the whole Church 'for ever.'

The Illumination had triumphed over the Jesuits.

## § 46. *The Omnipotent State*

If the ideas of the Middle Ages favoured the power of the Church, those of the Illumination implied an equally decided reaction in favour of the power of the State. Such a movement had already begun in the fourteenth century when the national State and the monarchies founded on it first arose. It made itself perceptible in the monarchy of Philip the Fair, and afterwards in those rights of superintendence and government which in the course of the fifteenth century the State acquired more and more throughout Europe. The State authority received a new and powerful support from the Reformation. The reformers (with the exception of Calvin and his followers) taught that no kind of external government should be intrusted to the Church, but merely the preaching of the divine Word and the administration of the Sacraments. The whole field of civic life was placed in the hands of the State, and even the government of the Church, so far as it involved the enforcement of external authority (in the enactment of laws, nomination to benefices, and Church discipline). The State was prepared to govern the Church by no means in Protestant countries alone, but likewise in Catholic territory. An idea was abroad which was not peculiar to the Reformation, so far as it was a question of the supremacy of the State over the Church, but rather one which the Reformation had inherited from the fifteenth century, and which henceforth from the sixteenth century onwards had attained full clearness and power throughout the whole extent of the West, in Spain and France, in Bavaria and Austria. Gallicanism, which ruled the Church of France from the sixteenth to the eighteenth century; Febronianism, which was defended with all the resources of his extensive learning by Justinus Febronius von Hontheim (suffragan bishop of Trier), in his work on *Ecclesiastical Constitution and Papal Authority* (1756), represented those spiritual tendencies which had grown up in the Church also, and which assigned to the State supreme authority of supervision, with direct power of interference, in some cases, even in spiritual things. The State revealed its inborn forces; and with an increasing consciousness of its own inherent power it claimed for its own the whole inner and outer world of culture. Here again the Illumination brought final and decisive change. Philosophical speculation on the origin and nature of political authority had led to the discovery that the State originated in a contract, known as the Social Contract (*contrat social*). This conception goes back as far as Aristotle. It had been already current in the Middle Ages. But now, for the first time, it unfolded the full power inherent in it.

According to this doctrine the Social Contract was concluded in favour of the State, and of no other authority, not even that of the Church, for instance. In favour of the State, and of the State alone, the individual parts with his natural freedom. It follows that all public authority belongs to the State, that all exercise of authority within the State can rest only upon contract and delegation on the part of the State. The authority of the State is omnipotent, and even that of the Church is only an outcome of it. Hitherto the whole idea had appeared to be mere theory; and this particular train of reasoning had remained theory for many a long century. But the Illumination bore within it a force which put fire to the gunpowder, and that force was the idea that the past has no power over the present.

According to the principles of the Illumination, the results of historical development are not binding, as such. They lose their binding power the moment their unreasonableness, or contradiction to the results of philosophical thought, becomes evident. The State is free to make the natural law of reason a positive enactment. Nay more, it is not only the highest right, but the highest duty of the State to realize this ideal by the removal of existing law. The State is all-powerful in opposition to the traditional order of law ; and the present age demands before all that the State shall establish this unrepealable law of reason, in all its power, in the place of historical law. So the State grew, and the wings of legislation waxed strong. The eighteenth century actually believed in the power of the State to put an end to all the asperities and imperfections of human society by legislation, and to re-establish a rational, universally just and perfect law that should bring with it happiness and freedom.

The world underwent a course of trenchant legislative reform, which swept away much that was already inwardly dead. The French Revolution was a magnificent attempt to order the world anew, and to reinstate the long-forgotten rights of man, according to the eternal, rational principles of liberty, equality, and fraternity. It was borne up by great hopes, and welcomed with deep and noble enthusiasm. By the Revolution, the power of the State, the power of the law, the incarnate Reason of the age was declared to be the mistress of the world. It lay with the Revolution alone to renovate the whole nature of legislation and of society, and to empty the cornucopia of happiness over a humanity delivered from the fetters of the past.

The Revolution ended in the Reign of Terror. The happiness it had dreamed of gave place to horror. Freedom disappeared in the despotism of a military autocrat. It became evident that even the State is not almighty; that, as a general rule, law cannot do whatever it pleases; that the sudden sundering from the past leads society not to heaven but to the abyss. The Revolution and its consequences swept through the world like a purifying fire; and then, after all, it left its work to be completed by the powers which had sprung out of the past.

In this energetic movement of reform the old aristocratic State, with its privileges and class distinctions, was overthrown, and made room for the democratic State founded on the equal public rights and duties of every member of the State.

Even the Church of the old order was swallowed up by the movement. From the second half of the eighteenth century the omnipotent State thought to mould the Church like wax in its hands. It was conscious of its vocation and free power to determine, not only the external position, but the inner life of the Church according to its own rational ideals. In this spirit Joseph II. began his legislative reform in the ecclesiastical field. He reformed the orders of the clergy by doing away with all that were not engaged in the work of the ministry or of education (1782); and he merged their revenues in a common 'religious fund' administered by the State. He reformed the culture and education of the clergy by establishing, in the place of the schools belonging to the Church, 'general seminaries' belonging to the State, which were to spread the spirit of the Illumination among the pastors of the people. He regulated the form of worship, the style and contents of the sermon, the hymns of the monks, and the decoration of the churches, both great and small. The whole field of ecclesiastical life was to be remodelled by him once for all, with a strong hand ; and, from his own point of view, the change was a suitable and rational one. But the reform ended in the Belgian revolution (1787), which cost Austria one of its fairest provinces ; and the work of Joseph had to be undone by another series of reforms.

The legislation of Frederick the Great, which determined the character of the Prussian Code (1794), was maintained in a like spirit. The Law of Prussia recognizes no general Church, either Catholic or Protestant, but merely the congregation, the 'Church society.' Several congregations, or Church societies (which, according to Prussian law, may or may not hold the same faith) form, not a Church, but a Religious Party ; something like the evangelical party, or the Catholic powers in Europe. No kind of common organization is pre-supposed in this arrangement, except that the Catholic Church societies are distinguished by the fact that several of them, which form the congregations of a diocese, have one president, the bishop ; while among the Protestants several societies are likewise subordinated to the same provincial consistory—an arrangement which is, however, purely accidental, as far as Prussian law is concerned, and rests, not on the constitution of the Church, but on that of the several local congregations (Church societies). The Church is divided into atoms. The Church, even the Catholic Church, is dissolved by law into a series of local congregations.

The only authority to which the congregation is subjected is virtually the authority of the State.   The King
of Prussia is the chief bishop and supreme authority in
both the Catholic and the Protestant Church.   'Foreign
superiors,' as, for instance, the Pope, may take upon
themselves no legislation, no jurisdiction, and no active
authority in relation to the Church of Prussia.   If the
Pope wishes to exercise his rights within Prussian
territory, he must nominate a native vicar, that is, a
subject of the King of Prussia.

This was the Church Law of the Prussian monarchy,
as the lawgiver evolved it out of his own reason ; and
he believed himself both justified and able to turn these
results of his philosophy into actual living law, by a
simple act of legislation on the part of the omnipotent
State.

The French Revolution advanced the farthest, even
in the field of ecclesiastical legislation, in realizing, by
means of a State decree, the free natural law devised by
reason.   The revolutionary Church law of reason and
nature is embodied in the 'Civil Constitution of the
Clergy' of 1790.   The constitution of the Church cor-
responds to the constitution of the State.   Every canton
has its pastor, every department its bishop.   The pastor
is elected by all the 'active' citizens of the canton,
without regard to their religious profession, just as the
bishop is elected by the 'active' citizens of the department.   For such a civilly constituted Church the Pope
does not exist.   Even creed plays no part in it, in so
far as every citizen of the State is as such a member of
the Church.   The Catholic Church in the traditional
sense has ceased to exist.   It is abolished by the law of
the State.   The State is now not only a State but a

Church, and ecclesiastical administration is a part of political administration. Consequently, the same corporation of electors which elected the organs of the State, that is, the District Council or the Departmental Council, is also empowered to elect the pastor or the bishop. The constitution of the Church is mapped out with lines and circles, drawn in strict correspondence with the constitution of the State. The living forces of the Church, the Papacy, and the traditional faith, are ignored. The State is free to deal as it will with the law of the Church and its existence. In the days of the 'Reign of Terror,' Christianity itself was actually abolished, if only for a time; and the worship, first of 'Reason,' then of the 'Supreme Being,' was introduced. The State ruled with unlimited power even over religion. Napoleon, by the Concordat of 1801, restored the Papacy and the Catholic Church to a place in French law; but, nevertheless, in that law, the foundations of which were laid by him, the great revolutionizing thought of the age of the Illumination—that the Church with its administration is incorporated with the administration of the State—is alive in France to this day. The unlimited authority of the State over the Church meant also its unlimited authority over the property of the Church. Joseph II. formed the State 'religious fund' from the endowments of the abolished monasteries. The French Revolution declared the entire property of the Church to be the property of the nation. The same advance was also made in Germany. The Peace of Lunéville, 1801, ceded the left bank of the Rhine to France. The German Empire thereby promised that the temporal princes who were dispossessed by the treaty should receive compensation out of the imperial revenues. The Church had to bear the cost of this compensation. The decree of the imperial commission of 1803 legalized the secularization of Church property (that is, of the endowments of all bishoprics, monasteries, and other foundations), and the abolition of the spiritual principalities. A death-blow was struck at the temporal power of the Catholic Church. The State avenged itself for the wrongs it had suffered in the times of the Hildebrandine system. Armed with the principles of eighteenth century philosophy, it overthrew not only the Jesuit Order, but the Church itself, both Catholic and Protestant.

## § 47. *The Idea of Toleration*

The permanent result of the intellectual movement which is comprehended under the one name of the Illumination is to be seen neither in the abolition of the Jesuit Order, nor in the supremacy which the omnipotent State obtained over the Church. The Jesuit Order was re-established by Pope Pius VII. as early as 1814. The age of the omnipotent State was by that time over. The lasting fruit of the Illumination—for no great intellectual movement passes away without leaving some such lasting fruit—consists rather in the principle of toleration, for which the Illumination succeeded in obtaining universal acceptance, and this chiefly in opposition to the Catholic Church. Intolerance is the principle of the Catholic Church. As, according to the Catholic faith, to be subject to Pope and bishops, that is, to belong to the body of the Catholic Church, is indispensable to the salvation of every individual soul ; so that Church considers itself, not only justified, but bound to reduce the heretic to subjection (by force, if necessary), and in extreme cases to punish obstinate heresy with death, as a heinous crime and dangerous to the commonwealth. Even the Protestant Church has had repeated fits of intolerance, and has condemned and punished the heterodox by means of the temporal authority. The most famous case of this kind is the execution of the Spaniard, Michael Servetus, in Geneva, (1553), on account of his Anti-Trinitarian doctrines, which was chiefly insisted on by Calvin.

The idea of toleration advanced step by step together with the Illumination. It was realized in the second half of the eighteenth century, in Germany by Frederick the Great, and Joseph II. in France by the Revolution. The Declaration of the Rights of Man (1789), which to a certain extent embodied the programme of the Illumination, proclaimed at the same time freedom of religious worship; and thereby it finally gave to the Protestants of France the toleration they had so long desired, which had been denied to them since the abolition of the Edict of Nantes by Louis XIV. in the year 1685.

Even in the nineteenth century the Catholic Church has given utterance more than once to its principle of intolerance, when, through the mouths of Pope Gregory XVI. in 1822, and Pope Pius IX. in 1864, it condemned liberty of creed and conscience. Nevertheless, the demand for that liberty, which excludes all external control over the religious opinions of the individual, is at the present day, without exception, granted in all civilized States, and likewise rules the opinions of all educated men, both Catholic and Protestant. And in this fact we see the great result of the intellectual movement of the last century; it is the final victory by which, in spite of all, the Illumination overcame external authority, more especially that of the Catholic Church.

The eighteenth century ended, and at the same time perfected, its greatest work in the destruction of the temporal power of the Church, both Evangelical and Catholic. Hereby a way was opened out for a future which was destined to regenerate the life of the Church by means of her own spiritual forces.

# DIVISION V

# THE NINETEENTH CENTURY

## § 48. *The Question*

THE nineteenth century was brought forth in the storms of the French Revolution. The whole world was in process of dissolution ; and not only the world without, but the intellectual world within. The Illumination had come, and it had taken heaven away with it; not only the visible heaven which the discoveries of natural science had turned into a mere optical illusion, but, what was more, the invisible heaven which the Christian faith had spread out, glorious and consoling, above the world of this life. The fixed, traditional theory of the universe which the Church upheld, and which in the time of the Middle Ages and even as late as in the sixteenth and seventeenth centuries had taken hold of the individual and guided him with a firm hand, safe and unharmed through life, had been destroyed by philosophic doubt. And together with the firm, religious theory of the universe, which ruled the moral life both of the individual and of society, the traditional foundations of Church and State were utterly destroyed. The consequence of the Illumination was the Revolution.

The nineteenth century was confronted from its birth with the question : Can that which is destroyed be

restored? Can its firm foundation be restored to an
utterly shattered society? Can there be given back to
it the faith which redeems and upholds the world—the
faith of Christ? According as it answers this question
will the fate of our century be. The history of the
Church in the nineteenth century is mainly occupied
with the answer.

## § 49. *The Restoration and Romanticism*

The Revolution had cost the French Church its
temporal possessions, for the property of the Church
had become secularized by the State. In Germany
also political events led to practically the same result.
The Peace of Lunéville (1801) had ceded to France the
left bank of the Rhine : but only the hereditary princes
thereby dispossessed were to be indemnified out of the
resources of the Empire. By this simple means the
spiritual principalities on the left of the Rhine disappeared. The disappearance of the rest also followed
on the final act of the Extraordinary Deputation of
1803, by which the Treaty was carried into execution.
The indemnification due to the temporal princes who
were injured by the Peace of 1801 was effected by the
abolition and partition of the 'immediate' spiritual
principalities and lordships of the Empire. With
regard to the ecclesiastical possessions which were not
'immediate,' that is, those lying in temporal territory,
the princes received full power to secularize them ;
a power which was exercised on the part of the Prussian
State by means of the famous Edict of October 30,
1810. The territorial princes promised an endowment
in place of the confiscated Church property. When the

storms of the Napoleonic age had blown over there was a rearrangement of ecclesiastical affairs. As in France, the Catholic Church had been re-established by the Concordat of 1801, and its organization and maintenance regulated anew; so, by a succession of treaties with the Papal court (in 1817 a Concordat was made with Bavaria, and in 1821 the Catholic Church of Prussia was re-established by the Bull, *De salute animarum*), the external organization of the Catholic Church was repaired in Germany also; the boundaries of the bishoprics and archbishoprics were laid down anew according to the new territorial boundaries; and the worldly condition of the Catholic Church was made secure by endowments from the territorial princes. The Evangelical Church did not succeed in obtaining a legal endowment secure from the caprice of the government for the time being. But even the Protestant Church was re-established in conformity to the present alteration, that is, the enlargement of territory; and in the national Evangelical Church of Prussia an ecclesiastical body appeared that was able to ensure room for the development of movements far greater in power and significance. In the second and third decades of our century the Revolution was followed by the Restoration.

At the same time the spirit arose which was to give an inner life to these newly created forms; the spirit of Romanticism—that powerful reaction of the nineteenth century against the ideals of the eighteenth—which signified, not merely a school of poets, but a wide and fruitful intellectual current which flooded far and wide the world of art and science, of Church and State. The eighteenth century was filled with the idea of the deification of the individual and of the free, conscious, utilitarian reason of the individual. The result was a Rationalism which only valued that which could be recognized as a means to an end; which conceived of religion and Church merely from the point of view of practical utility, so far as they produced morality; which denied everything miraculous as irrational; which disposed of Church and State in the most arbitrary and revolutionary manner, because no right to existence was conceded to the facts of history, but only to what could be conceived by the present age as subservient to some end. Against this individualism, with its preaching of liberty, conceivability, and rationality, already in a few great spirits of the eighteenth century a reaction had begun, the object of which was a return from illumination, from art and culture, to the power and simplicity of nature. It was Rousseau who opposed to the culture of his age his gospel of Nature; who thought to discover the ideal of humanity in the wilds of Canada; who taught his contemporaries to enjoy in solitude the sublimity and beauty of nature, the gold of the broom, the purple of the sun's rays, the majesty of high mountains, the splendour of the freeborn landscape, as yet untamed by the hand of man; who proclaimed, in opposition to the philosophy of illumination, the heart's ineradicable longing for the living God to be the indestructible first principle of all religion, and the incontrovertible proof of its ancient truths. In this powerful man, contemptible as he was in character, but great through the power of insight which accompanies the sensibility of genius, were united those ideas which were destined to bring forth, not only the Revolution, but the strongest reaction against it. His *Contrat Social* proclaimed the sovereignty of the people,

which in France destroyed first the royal power and
then both Church and State. His revelation of nature,
with all her secrets, her wonders, and her eternal forces ;
his admiration for the original power of the people,
untouched by any culture ; and at the same time his
defence of the claims of the heart against the logic of
the understanding, made him the originator of the
movement which regenerated Church and State. One
of the results of the influence of his ideas was a complete revolution in taste, which returned from the formal,
classical French style to Homer and Shakespeare, to
the true understanding of antiquity, and at the same
time to the fresh, eternal springs of national poetry.
Herder discovered the ballads and songs of the people ;
Goethe wrote his *Götz* and his *Werther* ; and the youth of
Germany sought in *Sturm und Drang* deliverance from
traditional forms, and a return to the eternal truth of
nature. From these beginnings in the eighteenth century
arose the Romanticism of the nineteenth. The individual,
and with him the reason of the individual, was dethroned.

What is the origin of law? The eighteenth century
answered : It is the conscious and deliberate choice
of the individual, when by free contract (*contrat social*)
he passes from a state of nature into the political and
legal state. The nineteenth century found through the
mouth of Savigny another answer to this great question :
Law originates rather in the national sense of law ; in
the unconscious, instinctive moral claims of the national
conscience, working by an inner necessity. The people
bring forth the law out of the darkness, imperceptibly,
inexplicably. The origin of law is a positive, historical,
mysterious, almost miraculous fact. And what is said

of law may be said of the State, of language, of art, and even of science. It is not the spirit and the conscious will of the individual that brings forth the whole of this ideal and social world in which we live, but the spirit of the people; it is the people's united force which unconsciously upholds the individual, bears him away with it, and overpowers him. The individual is not born to be the sovereign, but only the servant, the tool of the vast forces of history which surround him and which work in the movements of large masses.

A sense was awakened for something not made arbitrarily and by the will of the individual, 'sicklied o'er with the pale cast of thought'; a sense for something given, and authoritative, the result of slow processes of natural growth. The real world, with its forces, cast this binding spell upon a century satiated with reason, just because it had not arisen from the categories of the understanding; because it confronted the individual as something superior to him, and at heart incomprehensible. Not the intelligible and rational, but the unintelligible that was instinct with natural impulse; that bore the scent of earth about it, and spoke of mystery and adventure, romance and fairytale; the infantile and naïve and unconscious, this it was that Romanticism thought great and glorious; that the nineteenth century pursued with yearning, and set forth with fascinating power in art and science.

Under the stimulus of Romanticism arose the researches of the present day in philology and history, the present enthusiasm of Germany for nation and for State, and the reawakening of ecclesiastical life. The sun of the religious Illumination, which lighted up Christianity only so far as suited its own reason and

utilitarian ends, and left behind it nothing but a few
cold truths of the understanding, lost its splendour in
the clear light of day.  The nineteenth century desired
not criticism but conviction, the faith of its fathers, the
living bread in the place of which it had been offered a
stone.  The mysteries of Christianity found believers
again by the thousand.  The Reign of Terror with
which the French Revolution had closed ; the need
arising from the great military events which filled the
beginning of the century ; the higher moral impulse
which was given by the war of freedom, especially in
Germany, all these occurrences combined to plough
deeper the furrows in which the seed of the Divine
Word was again to strike root.

The Christian religion came, consoled, and quickened.
Upon an age of criticism and unbelief there followed
an age of yearning desire for revealed, historical, positive
Christianity.  Upon the tumult of freedom which came
to so fearful an end in the French Revolution, there
followed a more decided longing for some firm and
fixed authority ; upon an age of Illumination the thirst
for a faith that should have power to satisfy the heart,
and to give deliverance from the world and sin.

And so it came to pass that in the beginning of our
century the Catholic and Protestant Churches arose to
new life.  The Catholic Church was at once met by the
enthusiasm for the Romanticism of the Middle Ages.
For the Middle Ages were, before all, the time of the
people's naïve life ; the age of the natural and the
marvellous, and yet the age of the two great world-
ruling powers, the Empire and the Papacy.  Of these
two authorities, one, the Papacy, was still living.  The
powerful historic grandeur of the Papacy, the mighty

and authoritative fabric of the Catholic Church, the
pomp of Catholic worship which pressed all the arts
into its service, and gave wings to phantasy and
religious emotion, all this exercised over Romanticism
an irresistible magic. The Catholic laity burned again
with ardour for their Church; nay more, a great number of leading Protestant Romanticists, like Stolberg,
Phillips, Friedrich von Schlegel, Zacharias Werner,
went over to Catholicism. Romantic Catholicism began
its reign in Germany, France, and Belgium. It still
bore within it many eighteenth century ideas. It
sought to harmonize Catholicism with the philosophy
of the present (Hermes at Bonn). It had an inward distaste for processions, pilgrimages, the worship of relics,
and, before all, of the Jesuit Order. It held to a great
extent by the Councils of Constance and Basel, and
protested against the unlimited authority of the Pope.
In its heart it even regarded believing Protestantism as
a form of Christianity well-pleasing to God; and warm
relations were frequently entered into between Catholic
and Protestant believers. It was a moderate, or, as it
was later and rather inaptly called, a liberal Catholicism;
and it was filled with the conviction that the Catholic
Church and the modern State, with its liberty of creed and
conscience, that, above all, the Catholic Church and the
educational ideals of the nineteenth century represented
no irreconcilable opposites. It even believed that the
rights of freedom could be best defended and founded
from the Catholic side. All these views were combined
with what was in its essence decidedly and truly
Catholic. The Vicar - General, Wessenberg of Constance, represented, in a character of great significance
and far-reaching influence, a marked type of Romantic

Catholicism. Until the middle of our century this moderate form of Catholicism was the ruling one, and only then it was destined to be overcome by *Ultramontanism.*

Side by side with Romantic Catholicism arose a Romantic Protestantism. Its great work was to unite the two Churches of the Protestant confession. In Prussia the Union was carried out by order of Frederick William IV. (September 27, 1817). The Reformed and Lutheran National Churches of Prussia, while retaining their special confessions, were united in one 'Restored Evangelical Church,' the unity of which consisted in a common constitution and a common government, as well as mutual administration of the Communion of the Lord's Supper. Many of the National Churches followed this example, some by the abolition of the articles of confession, as was the case in Baden (1821). The active power which gave life to the Union was the widespread conviction that differences of religious confession (between Lutherans and Reformed) are unimportant, as far as the Church's life is concerned; and at the same time the feeling of the common opposition of all believers against unbelievers. Eighteenth century Pietism was yet alive in many classes however. Illumination might conceal it; and the Protestant Union was the significant result which it brought forth in the nineteenth century, now that it had undergone a new development in union with the intellectual current of Romanticism. It had accomplished, as of old, great things in the field of home and foreign mission; and, because it had abandoned its peculiar 'Pietistic' character, by giving up the ascetic forms of the older Pietism, it exercised in its new form of Unionism all the greater influence on the intellectual and ecclesiastical life of the present day.

It was an error to suppose that an essentially religious movement like the union of two Churches holding different confessions could be carried out by measures of ecclesiastical government alone; and the conflicts to which the Union gave rise have repeatedly made the gravity of this error evident. It was likewise an error if the difference of confession was held to have lost its meaning; this the future proved. Nevertheless the Union, springing as it did from the forces of a genuinely religious and Christian life, has brought forth far-reaching and beneficent results. Its work was to bring about the mutual influence of Lutheran and Reformed, which is the distinguishing mark of Protestantism in the present day, and to further the exchange of spiritual gifts, so that each might share in the other's wealth. The ideals which moulded the constitution of the Reformed Church, the self-government of the congregation by means of presbyters and synods, now made their way among the ranks of the Lutherans also; while, on the other hand, the dogmatic Christianity of the Lutheran Church, the supreme gospel of justification by faith alone, effectually reached the ranks of the Reformed.

Romanticism was the victory of the imagination and the emotions over the understanding. So far as Romanticism gave new food to the imagination, it was favourable principally to Catholicism; while, in rousing the forces of religious emotion, it was before all advantageous to the Protestant Church and to revived Pietism with its unionist tendencies, and strong endeavours after salvation, the last and greatest good.

## § 50. *Liberalism*

About the middle of our century, in the forties, Romanticism was destroyed by Liberalism.

Liberalism links on to the Illumination of the last century, bearing within it the same principles of Rationalism, but applying them differently. The difference lies chiefly in the field of constitutional politics.

The Illumination of the last century desired to lead the whole development of culture from a single starting point, and in one consistent spirit. The world was to be made happy in a particular way which was to be dictated to it by the State. In this sense Joseph II. undertook an 'illuminated' reform of the Catholic Church, by means of the coercive force of the State. In the same spirit Rousseau had desired to introduce an 'illuminated' state religion : whoever refused to belong to it was to be cut off from the State. The French Republic attempted to carry out Rousseau's programme by the introduction of a Church with a 'civic constitution,' that is, a Church without a Pope and without a creed. Everywhere it was the central political authority which strove to gain power over the whole intellectual life of the nation, and even over its religious life, as the State understood religion. The freedom of the Church was destroyed. On the same principles the abolition of the right of forming corporations, and other free unions, was undertaken. There were to be no more independent unions, no more societies and guilds, over and above the State. The State was all in all, the State was omnipotent. Although the Illumination started with the freedom of the individual, it practically ended in the despotism either of a monarchical or of a republican government. The Illumination was *illiberal*; together with religious and social freedom, it destroyed the most valuable expressions of individual freedom.

The Liberalism of our century arose from the influence of the age of Romanticism on the ideas of the Illumination. It was a compromise, on the one hand, between the freedom of the individual and authority, and on the other hand, between the power of associations and the power of the State.

Liberalism aims at the abolition of the omnipotent bureaucratic State and the establishment of a parliamentary and legal State in its place. In its reaction against the theories of the last century it produced that ideal of freedom in which and by which we all live at the present day; in this sense of the word we are all Liberals to-day.

The parliamentary principles of the present day require the co-operation of society in the government; in legislation (by Parliament); in government by means of the representation of provinces, districts, and communities; in administration of law by means of assessors and jurymen. Under these conditions the individual is at one with the authoritative monarchical government. A legal State, on the other hand, means that certain definite rights are ensured (in the last resort by means of judicial protection) to the individual, and likewise to the society. The idea of corporate freedom, as the most valuable expression of individual freedom, is revived in all its power. The eighteenth century had destroyed the corporate organization of society; the nineteenth century set to work to re-establish it in all departments. But the freedom and authority of the society had to conform to the modern conception of the

State. The society is to be free to conduct its own internal affairs; but there must be no longer any self-government of the corporation, such as was known in the Middle Ages, but rather internal freedom of the society under State supervision, with complete subjection of the society to the legislation of the State. The State is no longer omnipotent, but it remains sovereign : it is no longer the single authority which rules society, as in the eighteenth century, but it remains the supreme authority to which all other authority, even that of the corporation, is subordinate. The freedom which we all desire at the present day, and which we call the freedom of the individual, found its way into the world by means of the principles of Liberalism ; and in Germany it was the Parliament held in St. Paul's Church at Frankfort on the Maine, the Parliament of Professors of 1848, by which these principles made their triumphant entry into the public life of Germany.

The most striking instance of the application of the principle of freedom of union was the freedom of the Church. The Church was to be free to manage its own internal affairs, although it remained subject to the supreme supervision of the State, and to State legislation, so far as regarded its external legal position. While the eighteenth century had dealt with the Church as a department of the all-powerful State, it now once more received internal independence, and yet remained subject to the sovereignty of the State. The Prussian constitution of 1850 supplied the solution of the problem which from that time onward has governed the course of the Church's constitutional development; the Church shall regulate and govern her own affairs independently.

At this point of time begins the movement which in

the Evangelical Church aims at the deliverance of the
inner life of the Church from the authority of the State,
and at the re-establishment of an ecclesiastical constitution by which the Church is to be distinguished
from the State, and thereby given an independent
position.  King Frederick William IV. declared himself
ready to yield his ecclesiastical authority into the 'right
hands;' namely, as he himself meant, into the hands of
an Evangelical Church with an episcopal constitution,
subject only to the supreme guardianship of the
sovereign.  Yet all these plans of his remained 'mid-
summer-night's dreams,' as he himself rightly called
them.   The practical result which up till now has
followed from the movement, which aimed at nothing
less than the deliverance of the Evangelical Church,
may be seen rather in the presbyterian and synodal
organization which was carried out in the majority of
Evangelical Churches in Germany.  This has enabled
the representative bodies of the churches to influence
their government, and to aim at limiting the power of
the State itself over the Church, along with that of
officials appointed by the sovereign as supreme bishop.
This development cannot be regarded as having yet
reached a conclusion.  Even in our own time it has
attained a new and significant form in the Hammerstein
movement; and it will not cease so long as, in spite
of all outward presbyterian and synodal organization,
the purely political powers, the Prime Minister, or the
parliament, are the chief influences in the administration
of ecclesiastical authority.  It is a question of delivering
the Church, not from the sovereign as the supreme
bishop, but from the organs of a government which has
ceased to have a religious confession.  This movement,

which is without doubt justified in theory, would have more power and still greater prospect of success if it were not for the practical danger that the self-government of the Church, independent of the State, would be turned into party government. Here again the internal division of Protestantism is a hindrance to strong organization. Such party government would by no means always be the government of the orthodox Church party; and all party government, especially a change of party government, is fatal to the life of the Church. The part taken by the State in the government of the Protestant Church is a sort of neutral element which allows no one ecclesiastical tendency to obtain complete supremacy over the rest, and which obliges the ecclesiastical parties to conduct their warfare as they ought, not by means of the votes of synodal corporations and not by means of legal coercive measures, but with ideal weapons —with spiritual conviction and spiritual power.

The Catholic Church had no need to search for a constitution to free her from the State. She possessed such a constitution already; the magnificent product of nearly two thousand years of development, steadily advancing in the same direction. She seized immediate possession of the ecclesiastical freedom offered to her by the liberal opinions of the present age. In Germany and Austria, in France and Belgium, even in England, where since the year 1829 free room for development was granted to the Catholic Church, everywhere the State gave up its authoritative power over her, whether legal or practical; and as the Catholic faith gained new vigour everywhere, so the Catholic clergy obtained an authority undreamed of before; and the Catholic Church confronted the State with daily increasing power. In

Prussia, by means of the Constitution of 1848, the system of Frederick the Great laid down in the national law of Prussia was abolished. According to this law, the King of Prussia was invested with supreme authority even over the Catholic 'Church societies' of the nation; the Pope had no legal existence, and was cut off from all exercise of power over the Catholic Church of Prussia. By the Constitution of 1850 the Pope was reinstated in all his rights; and the freest action in its internal affairs was accorded to the powerful corporation of the Catholic Church. The reactionary movement of the fifties helped to the same end. The Catholic Church appeared as the stay of the government, as the born representative of the principle of legitimacy. The Prussian government made its peace with Catholicism; and what the Constitution of 1850 had begun was completed by the governments of the fifties and the sixties. As in Prussia Frederick's system was abolished, so in Austria that of Joseph was overthrown. In proclaiming the principle of ecclesiastical self-government, the Revolution of 1848 had already broken once for all with rigid traditional church law. The result was the Austrian Concordat of 1855 which delivered the imperial State completely to the Catholic Church, and declared the power of the Papacy, resting as it did on divine right, to be established by law.

The results which characterised the year of Revolution, 1848, were not only the full development of the modern idea of the State, and of the individual's right to freedom, but also a great advance in the authority of the Catholic Church and the reawakening of all its mediæval ideals of supremacy. It was an error of calculation, if, on the one hand, Liberalism believed that it could put the Catholic Church in full possession of her freedom of association, just like any ordinary society; and if, on the other hand, the governing powers believed that in the Catholic Church they had found their best ally in the re-establishment of a powerful and authoritative State.

## § 51. *The Realism of the Present*

The present age moves in the most diverging currents, yet all the varying expressions of its spirit have one thing in common—the endeavour to grasp, not merely conceptions, theories, ideals, but the living, actual forces that surround us, reality itself, that which is experienced as actually present and active alike in the natural and in the spiritual world. The Romanticism and the Liberalism of the first half of our century bore an essentially ideal and theoretic character. After an age of idealism we have entered upon an age of realism.

In the sphere of political life this realism finds utterance, before all, in the strong Conservative movement which is becoming ever more widespread. The Conservatism of to-day accepts Parliamentarianism and the legal State; but it recoils from the idolatrous worship which Liberalism, always a slave to its own theories, once brought to these its new creations. Parliamentarianism, that is, the co-operation of society in the government of the State, is regarded by every one at the present day as indispensable. But we have learnt that in these representative bodies too often the selfish interests of particular classes of society on the one hand, and political dilettantism on the other, play a prominent part. We have learnt that ‘representation of the people’ does not always mean that the people, that is, the State, is truly represented ; we have learned that always and in all ages the best, the worthiest, and the truest representation of the people is a strong Monarchy, the born helper of the weak and suffering against all the selfish tyranny of the stronger classes of society. We have learned that the art of government and the power to govern is never given to such assemblies, but always to the individual genius of the disciplined statesman, prepared for his office by the education of his whole life. The assemblies which represent society may prove a beneficent counterbalance, a wholesome check to the ruling authority, but they can never maintain a constructive, creative government, propelled by its own forces. Monarchy, with its officials, is and remains the real power of the State ; and the essence of Conservatism and its intellectual force lies in an experimental knowledge of the powers which alone can deal with the highest problems of the State. It is the same movement which in the field of political economy also has led to a departure from the purely abstract method of dealing with the economical freedom of the individual, and to a better knowledge of the great problems of monarchy and State which are here also awaiting their solution.

In the Evangelical Church the realistic tendency of the present day has given rise to the Confessional movement, which has made a decided and steadily increasing advance since the forties and represents a reaction, not only against the Illumination of the last century, but against Unionism which was equally determined by theoretic and emotional ideals. Her creed is the historical foundation of the Church, and at the same time a clear and intelligible expression of the truths derived from divine revelation which are living

within her.  A creed is not a series of dry formulas
summoning up the results of an abstract philosophical
science of divine things.  Rather, it is a record of the
divine truths which have hitherto sustained the life of the
Church, which through past centuries and even at this
day represent the source of the power and resisting
strength of the Christian religion against all hostile
influences, and are the principle of the continual regeneration of the Christian world.  It is this Gospel
and no other that has conquered the world.  The
Gospel, thrown into the form of a creed and lifted up as
a standard—the Gospel, witnessed and confessed before
the world, is in truth the ruling power in the Church ;
and the object of the movement was to make this
power once more supreme.  Within the Protestant
Church it was the Lutheran Confession, before all other,
which in large classes of the people had gained a new
consciousness of its own power, and new persuasive force
and spiritual energy.  The Union had been the direct
means of spreading its influence far and wide even
among the reformed in the united national Church of
Germany.  The creed was the banner under which the
Church of the Reformation had won its glorious victory ;
and now it was lifted up in the midst of the present
age as a sign that should be spoken against; but it
had power to awaken the fructifying forces of true
Christianity, and to win the heart of the people irresistibly
wherever it was represented by men of strong and
living character.  The difference which exists to-day
between the confessional movement, properly so called,
and the unionist movement, which had a more positive
tendency, is becoming almost imperceptible.  The Protestant Union also was firmly based on the Church's

confession as laid down in the Gospel. The liberal church party, following the realistic tendency of the present day, has likewise changed its character. At the present time the ruling tendency is no longer the philosophic and rationalistic one which stands to the substance of the Church's creed in the mainly negative attitude of the Illumination, a tendency chiefly represented in the Protestant Union. In the place of this old-fashioned liberal theology, there has appeared more and more clearly a historical tendency, which does not seek in the spirit of Rationalism to explain away the historic Christ, the glory of His character, and the power which has gone forth from Him; but endeavours in the course of historical research to give a secure position to the person of Christ, to understand Him, and to bring Him before our eyes. It is a tendency which approaches the magnificent history of Christianity with sincere reverence; and at the same time is careful before all things to seize on the kernel of religion which is believed to be concealed within the Church's faith, as the original substance of Christianity. The genius and force of this theology lies in historical research; its inward justification in its endeavour after truth, which it pursues for its own sake, untroubled by any doctrinal considerations whatever. But there is always a danger of the student becoming a historian, instead of a theologian; and of looking upon Christ and Christianity, not as facts which directly and personally concern himself, but merely as the great objects of scientific and historical investigation. But with most representatives of liberal theology at the present day the religious and ethical tendency is closely bound up with the historical. Even the liberal Protestantism of to-day does not commonly seek for the essence of religion in certain truths of the reason, but in the positive facts of the Gospel given in history, although it undertakes to define the substance of Christianity in a new manner.

So even liberal Protestantism, so far as it has advanced with any life and power, represents at this day the tendency of the new age towards the positive side of Christianity; and to this is owing the influence which even Liberalism has had in furthering the Church's interest and life. By the very means of historical research it has been able to exert a decided influence even on strictly orthodox Protestantism. It is Liberalism which, by applying historical criticism to the lesson of the New Testament, has strengthened the proof that the true surety of our faith is not to be sought in the formal letter of the word as such, but, as Luther once before sought it, in the Spirit of God alone which speaks to us with irresistible clearness and distinctness in the pages of the New Testament, giving testimony to the grace of God revealed in Christ, the Lord of glory.

Nevertheless the progress which the Evangelical Church has made in our time rests mainly and in the first place upon the confessional movement and upon the positive unionist movement described above. These it is which have accomplished the regeneration of faith, and thereby of the Church's life. These are the active forces which through so many centuries have led the Church to victory. It is they who have re-established the old faith, and which to-day as in the past work upon the heart of the people with healing and life-giving power. It is the spiritual power of this persistent movement in the direction of positive doctrine which has made it supreme in the Evangelical Church also. The two tendencies which still divide it, and which are still in many ways hostile, are not merely a source of conflict, for they also serve to correct and supplement each other.

Not only in the Protestant, but in the Catholic Church also there has appeared since the fifties a more and more decided tendency towards the historical side of the Church's confession. But the same spiritual tendency which revived the true spiritual life of the Evangelical Church in the Catholic Church led to Ultramontanism, with its imperious appetite for temporal supremacy; which knows of no concession to the modern ideals of culture and freedom; though it understands how to use in a masterly manner for its own ends, the rights of freedom offered to it by the modern development of politics; which, in short, no longer tolerates any relaxation of Catholic principles in favour of the modern State and of Protestantism, which to it means revolution and Antichrist. Ultramontanism is the intolerant doctrinal Catholicism which with its lust for power demands once more the complete subjection of the individual, of the world itself, to the supreme authority of the Church. The pontificate of Pius IX. (1846-1878) owes its historical importance to the fact that he made the ultramontane movement victorious, and destroyed romantic, moderate, and so-called liberal Catholicism. His ally was the Order of Jesuits (re-established by Pius VII. in 1814), whose ideals he realized. In 1864 was published the Bill of Errors (*Syllabus Errorum*) which condemns the modern State and modern liberty of faith and conscience. The decisive event which marked the victory of Ultramontanism was the proclamation by the Vatican Council (1870) of the infallibility of the Pope, of old the favourite dogma of the Jesuits. The dogma of infallibility means that the dogmatic decision of the Pope, as Pope, even without the consent of a general council, is binding on the whole Church when once the Pope has delivered judgment *ex cathedra*, that is, with the distinct view of instructing all Christendom on a question of belief or of morals. This dogma implies an endless series of propositions in which the infallibility of the Pope is maintained to be not only valid for the future, but to be an original part of the Christian creed throughout the past also. According to the doctrine formulated by the Vatican, all the Popes have been infallible, from the Apostle Peter (whom the Catholics hold to be the first of the line), down to the present day. Thus, for instance, Pope Boniface VIII. was infallible also, when in the year 1302 he issued his Bull, *Unam Sanctam*, which proclaimed to all Christendom the subordination of the temporal to the spiritual authority. By means of the dogma of infallibility the Gregorian system was revived, and the Church of the Middle Ages arose armed out of its grave to claim its ancient glory at the hands of the living present.

The moderate Catholicism of the first half of our century which maintained the compatibility of Catholicism with modern opinions, with the sovereign modern State and modern liberty of faith and conscience, was condemned to death by the Vatican Council by means of the proclamation of Papal infallibility. An outcry of terror rang through the educated Catholic world, especially in Germany. Romantic Catholicism was not dead yet. It arose against the new dogma which formal law now required it to believe. Its answer was Old Catholicism, which declared the Vatican Council invalid and the dogma of infallibility not binding. But it was in vain. The Vatican Council had fulfilled in every way the legal conditions of a general council. Its decision was immediately followed by the acceptance of the dogma in all parts of the Catholic world. The Church had spoken ; and to be a Catholic means to believe in the Church and her doctrine. The new dogma was invulnerable from the Catholic side ; because the doctrine of the Church's infallibility is the fundamental doctrine of Catholicism. The reformers had directed their powerful attack against this dogma, and delivered the Protestant world from the Church's formal legislative authority to enforce doctrine. Now at least it might be seen to what results the infallibility of the Church had led. The Vatican Council was the necessary consequence of the Council of Trent. If Catholicism in the sixteenth century had opposed the Reformation in order to take its stand exclusively upon the principle of the authority of the Church, this principle is the soul of modern Catholicism, and necessarily demands its full completion and development. Papal infallibility is the full completion of Tridentine Catholicism ; an infallible Pope is the incarnation of the authority of the Church, present every moment, ready every moment effectually to oppose the individual and his doubts, the present age and its criticism.

Directly after the Vatican Council, Alfonso de Liguori, the founder in 1732 of the Order of Redemptorists (an Order closely allied to that of the Jesuits), who as early as the year 1816 had been numbered among the 'beatified,' and in 1839 among the Saints of the Catholic Church, was admitted by Pope Pius IX. as one of the 'Doctors of the Church,' in the same rank as Athanasius, Augustin, Bernard of Clairvaux, and others (1871). Like the Jesuits he taught the Immaculate Conception of Mary, the infallibility of the Pope, and 'Probabilistic' morality (see p. 198). His promotion to the rank of a Doctor of the Church meant the restoration in our own time of the immoral 'morality' of the Jesuits, which was supposed to have met its judgment and its death-blow in the horror it aroused in the eighteenth and nineteenth centuries. The Probabilism of Alfonso da Liguori was of a rather more moderate kind. But even he sanctioned an act of sin in particular cases, if the doer has on his side not his own conscience—the opinion which justifies the deed may appear to him rather the less certain of the two— but grounds furnished by some writers on morality which counterbalance the grounds for the opposite opinion, a doctrine known as Æquiprobabilism. Liguori himself was an ascetic who exacted from himself the utmost rigour of asceticism. He went about in the poorest clothing, slept on a straw bed, and scourged himself daily till the blood ran. And this was the man who taught the 'Christian' morality described above. Could this be possible? It was possible, because the principles of monastic asceticism to which the Catholic Church held even after the Reformation declare renunciation of private moral judgment to be the highest perfection (see p. 181). Liguori took his stand by Catholic principle. He himself held that the securest plan was to subject himself in all things to his father-confessor, and to follow him as God himself; then the father-confessor alone bears all the responsibility, and

'God will not suffer a father-confessor to err.' Only from such a standpoint is subjection to external opinion—in contradiction it may be to a man's own conscience—at all conceivable. Marvellous as it may seem, it is nevertheless true that the libertine probabilistic morality of the Jesuits is a logical consequence of the ascetic principle.

It was a historical necessity that the work which began with the Council of Trent should end in the Jesuitic Ultramontanism of the present day.

The modern State was to be disturbed by the movement. In Austria, the Concordat of 1855 was revoked in 1870. In Prussia the 'Kulturkampf' began, upon the appearance of a decidedly ultramontane political party, which allied itself with the forces of opposition against the newly-founded empire. The Catholic centre was to be attacked, dissolved, and annihilated.

To this end war was declared against the Catholic Church, and that by attacking its least vulnerable point, its organization. This was a twofold error on the part of the Prussian legislation of May 1873, which, to fill up the measure of its mistakes, was forced upon the Evangelical Church also for the sake of 'Parity.'

The May legislation was a futile attempt to bring the spiritual office, and the training for it, together with its nomination and administration into dependence on the State, as if it were possible by law to change ultramontane Catholicism, which had grown up in the ranks of the Catholic clergy, into a kind of State religion. Every one sees the mistake now. The next ten years gave us a retrograde legislation, which so undertook the work of revision, that the May laws are so much waste-paper to-day. But the results of those laws are not to be so done away with. They are to be seen in the first place in the unbounded self-confidence of Catholicism. It has yet succeeded, and that mainly under the leadership of the 'peaceful' Pope Leo XIII. (after 1878), in overcoming the mightiest of modern states and the greatest statesman of the century. The storm of the conflict is past; but the troubled sea of Catholicism still heaves in huge wide-rolling waves. It has hope of overpowering Protestantism, first of all in Germany. A Catholic press has arisen that leaves no means untried to vilify Protestantism, and to represent Catholicism as the only stay of truth. The press is backed by a learned literature which, with equal determination, aims at the glorification of the Papacy and the abuse of Protestantism. It has borrowed its weapons from Protestantism. The very methods used by Protestant historians, rigorously true to original sources, are employed to refute the Protestant conception of history, and to prove rather that the Reformation has been the ruin, and the Papacy the salvation, of mankind. But in vain. Janssen's book merely proved that it is possible to heap up citations from original sources and yet to outrage truth.

Still more dangerous than this confidence of victory on the part of Catholicism is the friendly recognition which once more the Catholic Church has recently received from the State. In spite of all past experience the policy of the fifties with their systematic favouring of Catholicism is apparently renewed in Prussia. Now that the 'Kulturkampf' is over, the State has begun to pay decided court to the Catholic Church. Germany played her part by calling upon Pope Leo XIII. to be umpire in the question of the Carolines. Great was the homage which Bishop Kopp received when he treated of the revision of the May legislation. The tone of both the official and the non-official press, and, before all, the whole tone of the Government towards the Catholic press has been completely changed.

It is evident that the Protestant reaction will daily become stronger. It was the conviction that a battle must be, and that the great thing is to be prepared for it, which gave rise to the Evangelical Union which was joined by men of the most various positions in the Church; although unhappily it was not possible to effect perfect unity by this means. The same conviction was at the bottom of the Hammerstein movement which we have spoken of above. Its object was to bring about a purely ecclesiastical organization of the Church, and her deliverance from the supremacy of officials of the State, in order to make her more capable of carrying on the great work of her home missions, as well as the war with Catholicism, which is the part she must play in the history of the world.

But the hope of Protestantism lies, not in the Union, not in organization, but in the gospel of justification by faith alone. In this is the indestructible force of our Church, by means of which she will live till the end of time. Conflict will not be spared her; but conflict she fears not. With the proclamation of the dogma of infallibility, Catholicism has reached the highest point of its development. The principle of authority can go no further. Once this extreme height has been attained, a retrograde movement must necessarily follow; and the force which will bring about this movement is just this undue extension of the principle of

authority. We have seen the waters of Ultramontanism rise in the course of this century. They have
not been from all eternity; they are but of yesterday.
In the fifties they first grew greater and greater. As
they came, so will they go; and one thing is certain—
that they will be powerless against the Evangelical
Church; for our house is built on a Rock, even on
Christ our Lord.

## § 52. *The Church and Society*

If we look back upon the long course of historical
development, which, from the time of the Middle Ages
to our own day, has tended to strengthen the position
of the Church among the Great Powers of human
society, we shall see about the middle of our century
that a great period in the history of the relation
between Church and State comes to an end. Formerly,
when the State was yet in its legal infancy, it stood
in subjection to the Church as its ruler. That was the
age of Gregory VII. and Innocent III. Then, when
the State had attained its majority and become all-
powerful, it brought the Church into subjection—a
development which began in the fourteenth century and
reached its height in the eighteenth. First we see the
State ruled by the Church, then the Church ruled by
the State. Both these forms of the relation between
Church and State have ceased to exist. From the
middle of our century we note a movement which aims,
albeit with many a hard struggle, at the deliverance
both of the Church properly so called from the
authority of the State, and of the State properly so
called from the authority of the Church; and thus

sets up as its final goal a free Church in a free State. It is a movement which is favoured by the general development of societies; and the ideal for which it strives to-day is to combine freedom of social life with the sovereignty of the modern State.

The State is not the only power, not even the strongest power, with which the Church has to deal. Her actual position is dependent far less on the State than on the ruling theories of the age, the general course of culture and morals with which she is involved in continual action and reaction. Here is the field wherein the Church is called to develop her natural forces to the utmost, and where for her part also she feels most strongly the influence of other spiritual powers.

In this respect the present age displays a new character. The great spiritual tendencies which ruled the earlier centuries either proceeded from the Church herself, or were shared by her; so that in earlier ages she took her spiritual colouring from the current of the passing time. Thus in the Middle Ages, and in the time of the Reformation also, the spiritual tendency which gave tone to the age originated in the Church itself. Humanism, which for a period asserted itself independently of the Church, was drawn into the service of the Protestant Church by the Reformation. On the other hand, in the eighteenth century, the Church absorbed the Rationalism of the Illumination, and ministered in its turn to secular culture. We see first culture ruled by the Church, then the Church ruled by the culture of its age. Here again it would seem that the way is prepared for the great separation. The impetus which our century gave to ecclesiastical life is opposed by a counter tendency, which has become more and more powerful since the middle of the century, which is hostile not only to the ecclesiastical and Christian, but to every religious theory of the universe. This tendency, founded as it is not upon natural science (for upon such questions science can give no intelligence at all), but upon a philosophy of nature, has undertaken to draw a materialistic plan of the universe, from which God and Spirit have disappeared, and with them all that is presupposed in religion and morality.

While in the last century educated society, so far as its philosophy went, was still united in a common belief in God, freedom and immortality, to-day the educated classes are divided by a deep chasm. On the one side the Church's definitely Christian belief is once more a power, and a far-working power, before which the religion of the Illumination has disappeared. To this side belong all ecclesiastical tendencies: on the extreme right wing stands Catholic Ultramontanism, on the extreme left liberal Protestant theology. On the other side has arisen the unbelief which rules large classes of society, and more and more makes good its determination to destroy, not only the Church's faith, but all faith in a personal God, and to regard the universe as the result of a partly mechanical process of evolution.

This conflict of two opposing theories has already spread downwards from the educated classes among the masses of the people. This has given rise to the present situation, and on this depends the fate of the present age.

The history of the Church has always been the

history of the foundations of national morality. The
spirit of the whole development of Western culture is
reflected in the history of the Church. Tell me what
your faith is, and I will tell you of what spirit you are.
Tell me what your Church is, and I will tell you of
what spirit your people is. Not what man knows, but
what man believes, determines his worth and gives
power and substance to his life. The whole field of
morality is the field of faith, of those convictions which
can neither be proved nor referred to any motive, or
defended either by logic or by reason ; convictions
which are purely categorical, and enforce consent by
their meaning alone and not by reasoning. But it is
just these convictions which give strength of character
to the individual and the nation, and by which both
the individual and his nation lives. We live not by the
visible, but by the invisible, which the ear of man hath
not heard, nor the eye of man seen, neither hath it
entered into the heart of man to conceive it.

The history of the Church is the history of the past.
It will also be the history of the future. The history
of the Church is summed up in the proposition : that
the forces which determine the evolution of society lie,
not in intellectual knowledge, but in the religious and
moral life ; and that the power which is supreme among
all religious and moral powers came into the world with
Christianity.

### § 53. *The Situation*

To what shall I compare the society of our day ?

It is like the earth on which we live. A thin crust
around a great volcanic, seething, revolutionary heart of
liquid fire. Outwardly all is flourishing, and thriving in

peace and order; but another moment, and the Titanic elementary forces of the under-world have changed all this splendour into dust and ashes. There are only a few who form society, society that possesses, rules, enjoys, and takes a part in public life; the masses bear the burden of life, and at the same time represent the all-powerful enemy of society. So it has been in all ages. Society is wont to cherish the delusion that it constitutes the people, and that its interests are identical with those of the people; until some revolution shakes the earth beneath its feet, and shows it that it was not the people, but only the thin crust around the fiery seething heart.

In the Middle Ages, society was composed of only two classes, the nobility and the clergy. They alone possessed property and they alone ruled. Landed property (the only kind of property then recognized) was in their hands; and political authority then went with the possession of land. The nobility and the clergy were also the only educated classes; and outside their ranks was no independent culture. These classes were identified with the nation. The history of the nation was their history. The middle class was as yet incapable of intellectual action, and therefore also incapable of governing, and formed no part of society in the Middle Ages.

The German Reformation of the sixteenth century was the first great movement in which the citizens took a decided and independent part; and this was especially the case in Germany. In the German towns the Reformation made its peace with Humanism, and a national German culture grew up with the Lutheran Church and seemed destined to become the intellectual power that was to rule the future of Germany. But the Thirty Years' War put a sudden end to this development. The nation came forth from the terrible suffering of the great war in a miserably shattered and enfeebled state. It was reduced to economical and intellectual beggary. In the sixteenth century it had been the intellectual leader of the nations of the West, but now the sceptre was taken away from it. From the seventeenth century the culture of England and France took the supreme and foremost place instead of German culture. England was the home of that philosophy which produced the Illumination, and which was made the common possession of educated Europe by French literature of the eighteenth century. Even Germany became the pupil and the slave of the culture which she received from the hands of France.

But this culture bore within it the Revolution. The Illumination of the eighteenth century had made a discovery, the germ of which was already contained in the culture of the ancient world and in the Humanism of the fifteenth century—the discovery of man. It found that the fine clothes of the noble, and the cassock of the priest alike were only the covering for a man, for the same man that lurked under the citizen's coat, no better born, with no greater powers, no greater privileges than he. The ideas of liberty, equality, and fraternity arose and took the world by storm. They had always been there · Christianity more than all other had taught them. But now they became a power in public life; and the motive which now lay behind them was not love towards a man's neighbour, but hatred towards the privileged classes. The old order of society still held good; the power of the commonwealth was still in the hands of the nobles and the clergy, in France still more than in Germany. But the middle class had come to the knowledge of its full power. It felt itself to be the nation; it was the representative of the idea which ruled the century, the intoxicating idea of liberty and equality; and in that idea there was a new intellectual principle, a thought which finally raised the middle class to be the lord over society.

The ground trembled, and with one blow the social order which had ruled the West for a thousand years was annihilated. But why so suddenly? Why with such precipitate haste that nobles and clergy had not a moment to defend their ancient hereditary privileges? For this reason merely, because the ruling classes, the nobility and clergy themselves, were filled with the idea by which their power was to be destroyed. The leading ideas of the Illumination—liberty, equality, and fraternity—had sprung up in the *salons* of the higher classes, and it was they themselves who preached their own fall by means of their literature. The battle was already decided before ever a blow was struck; for ideas are what govern the course of history. The middle class found no opponent capable of resistance, because it merely carried into execution the judgment the ruling classes had already passed on themselves.

Since the end of the last century the middle class has gained more and more decided supremacy over the commonwealth. It forms society at the present day. Nobles and clergy are virtually absorbed in its ranks without distinction. It proclaims itself identical with the nation. It claims as rights belonging to the nation the functions which are granted to it by a constitutional government. The middle class thinks to defend the

interests of the nation in guarding its own, and so long
as its own rights are secured by the State it considers
that the nation's political development has reached its
goal.

Yet the middle class is not the nation. It is the
victim of the same delusion by which the nobles and
clergy were once deceived. The middle class composes
only ten per cent. of the population; it is confronted
by the ninety per cent. of the 'disinherited,' the whole
mass of the people. The middle class also is only the
thin crust around the enormous heart. The Proletariat
is the nation. The multitude, destitute alike of property
and education, is the nation. If the decision is by
counting heads, the rights and interests of the middle
class represent rather the very opposite of the rights
and interests of the nation. The people is the nation.

The people is already aware of its powers. Already
it has recognized itself as the real nation. The bat-
talions of the workers are about to form, that they may
thrust from its throne the middle class, the monarch of
the present. More and more clearly are shown the
signs of a movement, the aim of which is to destroy the
entire social order, the State, the Church, the family;
because all these supports of our culture and our
morality seem to the leaders of Anarchism to be so
many resources in the hands of its deadliest enemy,
the middle class.

Will the middle class be able to defend itself successfully against the onset of the people? Will we be able
to guard with a strong hand not merely our property,
but what is more, our religion, our family, our culture,
our liberty, against the insurgent masses? In other
words, will the Revolution of the nineteenth century

towards which we are drifting have another end than
that of the eighteenth?

One thing is certain, namely, that the issue will be
determined not by the bayonet, nor by any outward
means, but by the attitude which we and our society
adopt towards the great intellectual tendencies, the
ideas whose history will be the history of our century.

The nineteenth century also has made a discovery—
the discovery of Matter. It has found that Matter is
God. The whole marvellous heaven with all the starry
worlds which it contains—who has created it? Matter.
We ourselves, more wonderful still, full of inscrutable
powers and mysteries, bearing within us a world of love
and hate, of sin and of quenchless longing for the divine,
who has created us? Matter. Who is the guide of
our life, of our fate; who will determine our weal and
woe, our life and death; and who will sit in judgment
over them? Again and for ever it is Matter; the piti-
less, the implacable, forged by the iron law of necessity;
dead, unconscious, absolutely senseless Matter. The
world is not ruled by a conscious Will, but by the
unconscious; not by divine wisdom, but by perfect
unwisdom. It is a play of atoms and no more. Once
and for all the world is dead, and the sun has lost its
light. Take God from the world, and the world also
which bears us, which is akin to our spirit, and quickens
us with divine sympathy, has vanished together with the
living God. A whirling system of machinery is left.
Nay more, we ourselves are dead. Our life is an
illusion; our spirit does not exist; only the body is
left and performs its functions mechanically. It is not
a thinking thing but a phosphorescence, a will o' the
wisp. We are governed and determined, not by our-

selves but by the unchangeable laws of matter. We
were created by a mechanical process of evolution, and
by an equally mechanical process we shall be destroyed.
What are we? We are waves in the infinite sea of
matter, which heave but for a moment, only to disappear
again for ever. The whole world has become an open
grave, and we are already shivering in the universal
frost. A terrible morality is the outcome of this theory
of the universe, of this supposed discovery of the
nineteenth century; and already there is no lack of
voices which openly defend it. This morality runs so:
the struggle for existence is both the law of the universe,
and the law of evolution. In the struggle for existence
the small and the weak, those that are unworthy of
existence, will be destroyed, but the large and the strong,
who are most capable of existence and of a future, will
survive. The struggle for existence is the great refining
fire, which purifies the world from the presence of the
suffering and deformed. Therefore go forth into the
strife with your whole power. Make a path for yourself, and you will be the nobler, the stronger, and the
worthier for it. Go forth into the strife, and tread down
to the utmost the wretched and the small; and you too
will help to work out the one great problem of the
world's history. The powers of the individual are not
his that he may serve, but that he may slay his neighbour. Whoever survives in the struggle for existence
has right on his side. Might is right. The morality of
Christ is confronted by the morality of Antichrist.

Materialistic philosophy is capable of yet another
useful application. If there is no God and no spirit
and no immortality, then there can be no religion and
no morality and no law. How can matter be moral?

How can binding laws of right be given to atoms? Selfishness which gives strength to every individual in the struggle for existence, is the only principle that can be justified; and earthly happiness is the only goal of man.

It is this morality which makes materialism and atheism so popular; for it panders to the strongest instincts of the masses. And already this new Gospel of the nineteenth century has won believers. Already we hear the Marseillaise of labour :—

'We would be happy on earth alone, and suffer want no more !'

But in this Gospel lies the force of the popular movement against the middle class. It is the one idea most hostile to that class.

Shall we be able to resist a popular revolution? This question is the same as the former: shall we able to resist the materialistic ideas which, like a storm, are urging on against us the heaving masses of the people? The work of social reform, of economical legisation, at which we are labouring to-day, is doubtless of the greatest practical importance. But it is equally certain that the final decision does not lie here. The final decision lies rather in the ideas by which we ourselves are ruled, which we defend, but by which far more we are ourselves avenged, or rather judged.

Now it is certain that Christianity is such a conquering spiritual power, and takes us under its protection, so long as we unfurl its banner. But are we still Christians? That is the question with which we are brought face to face by the present age. According as we answer this question shall we pronounce our judgment. More correctly speaking, the question is this: Is modern society still Christian? Is the middle class still influenced by the world-conquering power of the Christian faith? As soon as we put the question we see how our whole fate hangs upon the issues of the moment. Whence, then, has the doctrine of materialism originated? From the ranks of the middle class itself. Where is it that atheism, veiled or unveiled, is most persistently preached? In the very ranks of the educated and well-to-do classes. Belief in matter, belief in atoms, has stifled belief in the living God; and the new Gospel of self-redemption through resignation and self-annihilation finds among the representatives of modern culture more reverent hearers than the Gospel—ancient yet ever young—of redemption through Jesus Christ. From the ranks of the middle class itself these thoughts have gone forth like a firebrand, stirring up the masses of the people against the middle class.

What is written in the books of the educated and the learned, this, and nothing else, is now preached in the street. Unbelief has grown up among us, unbelief which is kindling the revolution of the nineteenth century. And against this importunate unbelief no prophet has arisen amongst us, who, by the power of the Lord, might hurl into the abyss the mighty mass of lies. Thus, we are all of us, without exception, responsible for this state of things; and the judgment of our own sins hovers over us and our generation.

It is the culture of the nineteenth century which itself proclaims its own fall. Like the culture of the eighteenth century, so that of the nineteenth bears within it the Revolution. At the hour of birth the child which she has nourished with her blood will destroy its own mother.

So we stand at present. A thin covering divides us from the fiery abyss, and the spirits we ourselves have raised are labouring at our ruin.

It is now in this time when middle-class society is threatened by an implacable enemy, threatened still more by danger from itself, that the 'Kulturkampf' had to be fought, which called one half of society to take arms against the other. But among many classes, even in the ranks of the Evangelical Church, Christianity has become all the more living, all the more conscious of its power, through the conflict of opposing spirits which joined in the strife of Church and State. What seemed our ruin may prove to be our salvation. The 'Kulturkampf' is at an end. A battle of a more intellectual kind, the battle between Catholicism and Protestantism, between Christianity and Materialism, goes on unceasingly. But through battle the power of ideas is strengthened, and what we defend with our very life acquires a double worth for us. The great questions of religion stand out in the foreground of the public movement; and day by day, in the conflict of theories which is heard afar, summoning all to take a part in the struggle, the mass of the people learns once more the invaluable and imperishable nature of its Christianity and its Protestant faith.

Yet more. While the heaven of the present day is dark with the rising storm-clouds of social and democratic revolution, modern society must necessarily and naturally turn towards Christianity; for its golden sunshine still rests for ever on our whole earthly life, and warms, illuminates, and transfigures it. The situation is a serious one. The world understands that it cannot maintain its existence by means of mechanical skill, art, science, all the brilliant products of the human intellect. Even the world of modern society lives, not by bread alone, but by every word that proceedeth out of the mouth of God. In the terrible earnestness of our age, the powers of morality are revealed to the dimmest sight as the only forces which build the world and can uphold it and preserve it; they are the mighty pillars upon which our whole social life is resting. What mean the lightnings of the gathering storm of democratic socialism? What means the mighty, threatening murmur of discontent and of deadly hatred, which from the great masses of the people rises heavenward like thunder? They mean that the moral foundations of our social life are trembling. If the fabric of our social order is not founded on a rock, will it withstand the storm-wind that rages against it? It is a question of the regeneration of our whole nation. Where else can regeneration be found but in Christianity? It is a question of giving back to the masses of the people the sense that they belong equally to society, and have an equal interest in the maintenance of social order. How else is this possible save by the practical teaching of morality on the part of the ruling classes, the teaching of the same morality which is to be revived among the classes which serve? Be yourself filled with the brotherly love found in true Christianity, and then you will be able to pour out the same spirit on others also. Even to-day the promise is still given to Christian faith that it shall be able to remove mountains. The Christian faith which, by self-denial, overcomes all things in giving up all! The power of living personal Christianity is irresistible. Whosoever is filled with this power shall tear asunder the chains in which the world holds him captive, and shall become a lord over all things. Our age is put to the test. Is modern Christianity a Christianity in word only, or also in deed? Nay more, is it a Christianity of almsgiving only, or a Christianity which actually condescends to men of low estate, which reaches a hand to them as brothers, and secures and furthers their interests as its own? By this it may be seen whether the spirit of Christ lives in a man. The problem is not one which is directly given to the Church, as a Church, to solve. It is not a question of a Church, but a question of Christianity. You will only overcome the power of hate, if you are yourself overcome by the love of God through Christ.

From the beginning of this century to our own day a single upward movement has sustained the principles of Christianity and the Church. In many ranks of educated society Christianity is still living, consciously or unconsciously. In spite of all that Darwinism and Materialism have contributed to our culture, Christian ethics are still the supreme power in our moral life. Modern society has not yet ceased to be Christian. Nay more, the positive belief of Christianity has once more gathered together an army of followers under its standard. All may yet be saved. But one thing is certain: It is not our culture that will save us, but the Gospel alone.

# INDEX